ASPERGER SYNDROME AND

ANXIETY

By the same author

Asperger Syndrome and Bullying
Strategies and Solutions
Nick Dubin
Foreword by Michael John Carley
ISBN 978 1 84310 846 7

Asperger Syndrome and Employment DVD
A Personal Guide to Succeeding at Work
Nick Dubin with Gail Hawkins
ISBN 978 1 84310 849 8

Being Bullied DVD
Strategies and Solutions for People with Asperger's Syndrome
Nick Dubin
ISBN 978 1 84310 843 6

ASPERGER SYNDROME AND

ANXIETY

A GUIDE TO SUCCESSFUL STRESS MANAGEMENT

FOREWORD BY VALERIE GAUS

Jessica Kingsley Publishers
London and Philadelphia

First published in 2009
by Jessica Kingsley Publishers
73 Collier Street
London N19BE, UK
and
400 Market Street, Suite 400
Philadelphia, PA 19106, USA

www.jkp.com

Library of Congress Cataloging in Publication Data
Dubin, Nick.
  Asperger syndrome and anxiety : a guide to successful stress management / Nick Dubin.
      p. cm.
  Includes bibliographical references and index.
  ISBN 978-1-84310-895-5 (pb : alk. paper)
  1. Asperger's syndrome--Psychological aspects. 2. Stress management. 3. Anxiety. I. Title.
  RC553.A88D829 2009
  616.85'8832--dc22

                            2008042686

British Library Cataloguing in Publication Data
A CIP catalogue record for this book is available from the British Library

ISBN 978 1 84310 895 5

Printed and bound in the United States by
Thomson-Shore, 7300 Joy Road, Dexter, MI 48130

FSC
www.fsc.org
MIX
Paper from
responsible sources
FSC® C013483

To my late grandfather, Sydney Solomon
(1914–2002) and to my parents, Larry and Kitty.

Acknowledgements
I wish to thank my parents, The Gray Center, Janet Graetz, The Judson Center's Autism Connections, The Asperger Society of Michigan, The Michigan School of Professional Psychology, and Barbara Bloom for her fantastic editing job. Special thanks to good friend Katie Kramer for all of her support. I would also like to thank some family members who have been very supportive of me over the years: Uncle Howard and Aunt Susie, Cousin Art, Grandma Clara, Aunt Mary, Aunt Marion and Great Aunt Bertha "Boodie" Gross.

Contents

Foreword

As a psychotherapist, I have spent the last 15 years serving adults on the autism spectrum, mostly people diagnosed with Asperger syndrome and high-functioning autism. Anxiety is at the core of the problems presented by almost every client I have served. Until this book, there has been no self-help resource I could refer them to that dealt exclusively with the anxiety that comes hand in hand with adult Asperger syndrome.

There are several reasons why this book will be an invaluable resource to you and why I look forward to recommending it to my clients. The first is that Mr. Dubin bases his suggested strategies on two equally important sources of information, which he artfully integrates throughout the book. One is the psychology literature on evidence-based practice. The other is personal experience (the author's as well as others as featured in multiple vignettes) coping with the anxiety that comes with Asperger syndrome. Mr. Dubin's knowledge of both allows him to bring you this unique guidebook for navigating the challenges you may be facing in your daily life.

The second reason the book is so valuable to me and my clients is that it embodies a theme that has been extremely important in my work for many years: *acceptance.* As a cognitive-behavioral therapist, I am frequently helping clients to challenge maladaptive beliefs they hold about themselves and others. A major misconception that many people have about cognitive-behavioral therapy, however, is that we therapists are simply trying to get clients to "think positive" and focus attention away from negative things. In reality, there are often unpleasant truths that have to be examined and accepted before someone is really free to embrace the positive things that are in one's life. This is something that Mr. Dubin illustrates beautifully and consistently throughout the book, giving example after example of ways to accept the hindrances and pain that life can bring. He also offers guidance on differentiating the obstacles that are unique to Asperger syndrome from those that are universal to all humans.

Which brings me to the third reason I think you will be helped by this book. Mr. Dubin shows you that Asperger syndrome is not a disease or a defect, but rather a set of differences. Those differences, while making you anxiety-prone, also bring unique talents and strengths. Once you let go of the shame many feel about having the diagnosis, you will have more energy to explore your strengths and share them with whoever you choose. That is the true meaning of empowerment, and that is the gift Mr. Dubin has brought you with this book.

Dr. Valerie Gaus

Valerie Gaus, PhD, has been a practicing cognitive-behavioral therapist since she received her doctorate in clinical psychology in 1992. Currently she maintains a private practice on Long Island, NY, and serves as the staff psychologist for Vincent Smith School in Port Washington, NY. Dr. Gaus is on the advisory board of the Asperger Syndrome and High Functioning Autism Association, the grant review committee of the Organization for Autism Research, and the adjunct faculty at Long Island University/C.W. Post. She was also a founding board member of the New York Metro chapter of the National Association for the Dually Diagnosed.

Introduction

Assume, for the moment, that you were an alien looking into the possibility of becoming a citizen of the planet Earth. If you studied this planet, you would learn quite a bit from watching the ways human beings behave. You would observe human beings displaying positive and negative emotions: love, hate, fear, jealousy, rage, compassion and many others. You would be horrified to see some people on this planet are homeless and hungry, while others live in opulent homes and consume lavish meals. You would witness thousands of violent acts that frequently take place in war zones as well as cities and suburbs. As an alien, you would see that life is very stressful. Who in their right mind would want to live here?

But wait a minute! As a prospective citizen, you would also learn you have the opportunity to acquire personal power and live a life of dignity and self-worth and perhaps even make a positive difference on the lives of others on this planet. It would actually be possible to leave this planet in a better place than it was before you joined it. You would see human beings engaging in loving, compassionate, and creative acts. Looking at the totality of evidence, you would probably discover many reasons to come to live on this planet while acknowledging that life does involve its fair share of suffering.

Like it or not, here we are, without having the opportunity to contemplate whether we should journey from some other place. Our lives have extraordinary potential in spite of all the greed, selfishness, and injustice that exist. But for people with Asperger syndrome, life becomes even more of a challenging proposition than for "neurotypicals". People with Asperger's actually do feel like aliens on this planet. On a daily basis, we must fit into a world that seems totally foreign to us. This process of integration can be both exhausting and frustrating, but more importantly, it can provoke uncontrolled anxiety.

One reason I wrote this book is to affirm that anxiety is not a unique response for those of us with Asperger's and it contributes to our feeling like strangers in a strange land. If we are honest with ourselves, most of us will admit the world is a fairly terrifying place. Think of the uncertainty each of us faces all the time.

Our livelihoods are questionable unless we can find and maintain gainful employment and meet our daily and long-term needs. Dating and socializing are also major challenges as well, sometimes compromising our ability to form families and create social networks. These challenges, along with many others, present a serious handicap for many of us with Asperger's, but they are not insurmountable. As you read this book, I am going to be your personal guide in helping you think about how to meet some of these challenges more effectively. If you can learn to control your reactions when faced with these types of challenges, you stand on higher ground in accomplishing your goals and living a satisfying life.

If you are like me, you are tired of the generalities and platitudes about how to become less anxious. While some common-sense advice about and techniques for stress reduction can be helpful from time to time, often you need more substance. This is the first book on anxiety and stress geared toward individuals with Asperger's. Anyone interested in learning about what it is like to have Asperger's and the attending issues of stress and anxiety that can complicate the normal challenges of life will want to read this book. I recommend this book for parents of teenagers and adults with Asperger's, as well as teachers, professors, psychologists, psychiatrists, social workers, and anyone else who seeks a better understanding of people with Asperger's. After all, the better neurotypicals (non-autistics) understand our journey, the more acceptance and support we will receive from them.

No person, including this author, is immune from stress. I don't think it's possible for anyone to live without any stress, as stress can serve to motivate and inspire. I will do my best to present effective strategies that can be used to manage and substantially reduce your stress so that anxiety doesn't limit your opportunity to pursue goals in your life.

You may be wondering what compelled me to write this book. The reason is very simple: I know what it feels like to be hounded by the ever-present feelings of anxiety and panic brought on by life's usual challenges. I want to try to help others with Asperger's who may be confronting similar feelings. Encountering stress and anxiety has been a significant and lifelong issue for me. Working toward my doctorate in psychology, I have read a significant number of books that have helped me understand anxiety from psychological, medical, and holistic perspectives and have made my life less stressful and more peaceful. Today, thanks to hours of therapy, my studies, and the help of caring professionals and family, I am a far less anxious person than I used to be. Now, when stress and anxiety arise, I know how to deal with them more effectively. I don't pretend to live a stress-free life, but rather I face my anxiety head-on.

You might also be interested to know I was diagnosed with Asperger syndrome at the age of 27 in 2004. Understanding the Asperger's diagnosis was enormously helpful, because it allowed me to understand the source of much of my anxiety. For people with Asperger's, anxiety is often symptomatic of and aggravated by the neurological difference. I have yet to meet a person with Asperger's who does not experience a high degree of anxiety in his or her life. This fact is supported by the research I will be providing along with my own experiences.

Perhaps becoming aware your anxiety is a neuorological issue versus a psychological one can relieve a burden you've been carrying around for a long time. Maybe you've judged yourself harshly for the anxiety you regularly experience. Perhaps you've been told by others if you would just learn to relax, the anxiety would go away. Well, it's not that easy. Over a period of time, the anxiety-filled memories from childhood become locked in our brains, tending to make the anxiety stick with us through-out our lives. Anxiety, like rust, is difficult to get rid of. You can't just wave it away with a magic wand. It requires a lot of focus and hard work. If you are willing to put in the time, however, I believe the rewards will be far greater than you could have ever imagined.

If you could watch a videotape of me when I was in middle school, you would see one very anxious and self-conscious boy. I lived in a constant state of fear. What was I afraid of? Virtually everything. I was afraid of being criticized by my teachers (as I often was); scared of being bullied and teased by my peers (as I often was) and terrified that I would forget to bring home an important math assignment that was due the next day (as I often did). In essence, I saw the world as a very threatening place. At any moment, I sensed impending doom. Someone was going to humiliate, belittle, criticize, or scold me for something I did. Many of my fears were based in reality so I had good reason to be anxious.

As I grew older, I continued to be just as anxious, even though the conditions in my life had improved significantly. I no longer was a middle school student, nor was I the daily victim of bullying. By the time I entered college, I was doing fairly well academically and I was no longer being criticized for a lack of effort as I had been in the past.

However, certain challenges remained. I still struggled in various areas of my life. At various jobs I had, I was occasionally criticized for making mistakes and lacking social skills. Nowhere were my shortcomings more noticeable than when I failed a student teaching assignment in a second grade classroom. My cooperating teacher, who supervised my performance in the classroom, reminded me of my actual second grade teacher who was always critical of my performance. I found myself unable to accomplish even the simplest tasks. For example, I accidentally broke the school's expensive laminating machine; I often forgot to accompany the children from their gym or music class and walk them back to my classroom; I didn't reprimand students who were behaving badly, thereby failing to control the classroom; and I unwittingly engaged in inappropriate conduct. One day, I came to school wearing a sweatshirt I had bought at a jazz club when I visited Los Angeles a few years back. The sweatshirt had a picture of a martini glass and an olive on the back of it. You can imagine the looks I got from the principal and my cooperating teacher when I entered the building that day. I had no idea that I was doing anything wrong.

Being in that second grade classroom as a student teacher instantly transported me back to when I was a second grader myself. My face was constantly flushed from feeling constant humiliation and I was always sweating from the stress I was experiencing. It was exhausting. One day after school, my cooperating teacher actually caught me napping in a fetal position on the classroom floor. Stress can sap the energy right out of you. What I was experiencing as a student teacher was an example of a post-traumatic stress disorder. This may sound odd since this syndrome (which I will describe in greater detail in Chapter 1), is usually associated with returning war veterans, but it has broader applications with the Asperger population. I will spend some time talking about traumatic stress later on, but for now, you should realize this disorder is the manifestation of what happens when traumatic experiences lock into our memories.

Although I am far less anxious today, this change didn't happen overnight. It has taken a lot of self-awareness and insight to propel me to this place. I believe the same can be true for you, as well.

Stress management for an individual with Asperger's is a three-pronged approach:

1. You must understand how having Asperger's has contributed to your high levels of anxiety. You can't truly understand why you are so anxious unless you bring Asperger's into the equation. That's how this book is going to be different from anything you have previously read about anxiety. You are going to penetrate the mystery of why you have experienced such a high degree of anxiety for so long.

2. You must understand the manner in which you personally respond to stress and anxiety, i.e. your modus operandi in confronting stress. I am going to put forth a set of self-help tools based on cognitive-behavioral therapy that will assist you in monitoring your cognitions (thoughts) because sometimes thoughts that aren't adaptive explain the underlying causes of anxiety.

3. I am going to present an array of proven strategies, some of which have been shown to be tremendously effective with the Asperger's population and some that have been demonstrated to be quite helpful for the general population. You may not initially agree with all of the strategies I present. All I ask is that you keep an open mind.

Since people with Asperger's typically like to know what the future holds in store for them, I am going to summarize the contents of this book, chapter by chapter.

In the first chapter, we are going to look at the physiology of the stress response and the cognitive mechanisms that enable you to experience the feelings of stress. Our thoughts have incredible power when it comes to making us feel stressed. Thoughts can even influence how our bodies respond to stress. I will explain why that is the case. You are also going to learn how your brain and body are involved in controlling and mediating your stress as well as the dangerous medical consequences that unchecked stress can pose. It's extremely important to understand and recognize the underpinnings of our stress response because without that knowledge, your stress will go unchecked. If you have no idea how your brain processes stress and how it delegates responsibility to the rest of the body, you will not understand how to take conscious control of your own stress management.

The second chapter confronts the perennial question of why and how Asperger syndrome contributes to increased levels of stress and anxiety. After you finish reading Chapter 2, you will be aware that having Asperger's predisposes you to having fewer coping mechanisms. This reality makes it more predictable you will experience a great deal of anxiety. My aim in presenting you with this information is so you won't continue to browbeat yourself for your high levels of anxiety or attribute this condition to a psychological deficiency. It is not your fault.

In Chapter 3, we begin delving into the stress response in more detail. Specifically, I will introduce cognitive-behavioral therapy (CBT) and an offshoot of CBT called schema therapy. Several practitioners and researchers have shown CBT to be effective for our population. You will learn the basic tenets of this therapy and how the concepts of this therapy can be applied to your life. You will be able to evaluate whether or not CBT might be helpful for you in reducing your stress.

In Chapter 4, we continue to talk about schemas and relate them to an important concept called mindfulness. I will discuss ways to keep your attention focused on the present moment as opposed to the past or future and how this strategy greatly reduces the amount of anxiety you may be experiencing.

In Chapter 5, we look at relationships and the challenges they pose for people with Asperger's. More specifically, we'll look at what triggers your anxiety in dating situations and what you can do to lower this anxiety.

Chapter 6 provides an opportunity for self-evaluation of how you react to stress in the workplace. As with the previous chapter, you will be able to look at some of the triggers involved in creating stress and anxiety, then focus on your reactions to these stressors or triggers.

Chapter 7 considers professional therapists and therapies. We'll explore what kind of attributes to look for in a therapist. Furthermore, we'll set forth a list of different therapies so you have some knowledge as to what might be the best approach for you. I'll also tell you what kinds of therapists to avoid and how you can make that determination based on your own personal preferences and emotional needs.

The focus of Chapter 8 is meltdowns (seemingly uncontrollable outbursts with no obvious antecedants). We will examine why they arise, ways to control them and if there are any benefits to having them. You will see meltdowns usually occur when you feel a sense of chaos while simultaneously trying to create order. One of the main points of this chapter is that most individuals with Asperger's have an inherent urge to create order from chaotic circumstances.

In Chapter 9, we'll look at the correlation between shame and higher levels of stress and anxiety. I will introduce you to Carl Jung's concept of "the shadow" and how it influences us. The shadow is a mysterious subpersonality within our psyche whose level of influence extends beyond our normal conscious awareness. The shadow is our "dark side", the side of us we wouldn't even want our dog to know about. Becoming aware of your shadow helps you gain self-acceptance and a greater appreciation of your humanity. We all have this as part of our personality and must integrate and accept it as a part of our being if we are ever to make peace with ourselves.

In Chapter 10, we will discuss the vital roles of exercise, diet, and medication when reducing anxiety levels. There is a consensus among scientists that exercise does lower stress levels by releasing chemicals within us called endorphins, which is like the body's own morphine. This is what I call a good way of getting high. We will also explore the mind-body connection, and how anxiety can act as a destructive force throughout the body.

In the last chapter, we will try to examine anxiety from a spiritual perspective.

Just one caveat before we officially begin: the advice and information in this book is not meant to replace professional care. If you feel your anxiety has reached a point where you need professional psychological or medical treatment, this author advises you to seek it out and use the book in conjunction with your doctor's advice.

Let's begin to explore the most important possessions we own: our bodies and our minds.

Chapter 1

How anxiety works and ways to control it

"Just relax." How many times has someone given you that piece of advice? Aren't you sick of those well-meaning neurotypicals telling you relaxing is as simple as counting from one to ten? Stress management is not easy, but you can achieve it. However, you can't really begin to control your stress until you understand how it affects your life.

Stress is a complicated phenomenon that encompasses several different components. Much of this chapter will explore the physiological components of the stress response—meaning how your body responds to stress. There is also a cognitive component to the stress response, how you mentally process the stress you are experiencing. Most of this book will focus on the cognitive component of stress since it is so crucial for people with Asperger's, but you should realize that both the physiological and cognitive components are equally important and interdependent. How you respond to stress via the thoughts you tell yourself will affect your physiological reaction. If you tell yourself you are scared, your sympathetic nervous system will set your heart to beat faster and you'll start sweating. Likewise, your body's reaction to stress influences your thoughts. For example, you touch the scorching stove and before you have time to think, "That was hot," your hand does the thinking for you by reflexively jerking away. A few seconds later, you consciously think, "That was hot."

Let us begin our exploration by coming up with a couple of good definitions for psychological stress.

What is psychological stress?

Hallowell's definition of psychological stress

Although all human beings experience stress differently, some elements of stress are universal. To paraphrase attention deficit disorder expert Edward Hallowell (1997), *psychological stress results when a person feels vulnerable when confronted by a source of power.* This definition of psychological stress is extremely profound because it has marked implications for the Asperger's community.

Many of us with Asperger's live our lives feeling incredibly powerless. We feel as if we aren't on equal footing with everyone else. Somehow, social situations seem to get the better of us. Here are two commonplace examples that give people with Asperger's the jitters:

1. You go into a job interview with the expectation that you are going to be rejected by your potential boss because you lack social skills.

2. You go on a date convinced you are going to make a fool of yourself because you will engage in some socially inappropriate behavior.

If a person lacks confidence with his or her social skills, it means that he or she will put others on a pedestal in social situations, e.g. "the boss" and "the date" from the previous examples. Another example would be if I were to play tennis star Andy Roddick in front of 20,000 people on international television, I would obviously put him on a pedestal because of my awareness that he is a superior tennis player to me. In turn, I would feel powerless and hopeless in terms of winning the tennis match. The same principle applies to social interactions. When you habitually put people above you, you unwittingly give away your power to them. If you are constantly belittling yourself as being inferior to others, you automatically give away your power to those people and increase your own feelings of vulnerability. If you don't learn to reframe or change your thinking when it comes to your self-image, you will continue to feel powerless and vulnerable.

Easier said than done, right? We all know that to be successful in the world, it helps to have good social skills. I would be willing to bet a lot of anxiety is caused by our equating our social skills (or lack thereof) to our degree of success. Being under everyone's watchful, judgmental eyes can't help but make you feel vulnerable and powerless. Or can it? I propose that even though you may face most situations with the disadvantage of having unconventional social skills, it is still possible for you to work on reducing your levels of anxiety.

Reducing anxiety through healthy compensation

According to Alfred Adler, the founder of individual psychology, all human beings experience basic feelings of inferiority (Ansbacher and Ansbacher 1964). Since inferiority subsequently leads to feelings of powerlessness, humans attempt to strive for superiority by covering up the unwanted feelings of being inferior. This is sometimes referred to as "putting on a game face". We accomplish this objective by striving for achievement in other areas. This behavior is called unhealthy compensation or overcompensation, which we will talk about shortly.

Healthy compensation, on the other hand, doesn't try to remedy what's making you feel inferior. Instead, you compensate to better yourself as a person, knowing you have intrinsic value as a human being. Healthy compensation is akin to wearing corrective lenses to see better or employing the use of a hearing aid to improve hearing. We do not judge someone who needs these devices because they are compensating for something that is beyond their control. Furthermore, the fact that someone may not have 20/20 vision or good hearing has nothing to do with the quality of that individual as a human being. The same principle is true for issues relating to Asperger syndrome. Removing the cloud of negative judgment you inflict upon yourself will do wonders for your ability to take affirmative action and compensate in a healthy manner in areas in which you may have some weaknesses. If someone felt guilty about wearing glasses because he felt he should see better without them, wouldn't you try to talk some sense into him?

If you know socializing will never be a strong suit for you on the job, it might just mean you will have to go out of your way to be an exceptional employee in other facets of your work, such as being dependable, innovative, and trustworthy. When you demonstrate other positive traits, you reduce the powerlessness you feel at work because you have an intrinsic sense of self-worth in other significant areas; regardless of your social skills or lack thereof. You can then free up the energy you have used to berate yourself for having poor social skills by working toward developing those attributes that you're inclined to be naturally good at.

If an employer fires you for being socially incompetent but in all other respects you are an exceptional employee, he or she isn't a person worth working for. Furthermore, if you were healthily compensating in this instance, you wouldn't personalize and belittle yourself for your boss's arrogant behavior for firing you; instead, you would know that you have intrinsic value with or without your boss's approval. From a cognitive point of view, you would reframe this situation by telling yourself that there are probably many other bosses out there who would value dedicated and dependable employees, who do not have the best social skills. This thought would reaffirm your self-worth.

Here's another example of utilizing healthy compensation to reduce anxiety applying a similar analogy. Assume you are having some difficulties on the job because the boss is asking you to do a lot of multitasking. As someone who has some self-awareness, you intuitively recognize that multitasking is a weakness, whereas intense focus and concentration are your strengths. If you remained silent, and did not inform your boss of your inherent limitation and tried to weather the storm, you would continue to be anxious over your poor job performance while never getting a true chance to utilize your strengths. However, if you made up a disclosure script (Hawkins 2004), which is basically a written monologue, this information would suggest that your boss should re-focus your assignments if he or she is really interested in getting the best work performance from you. Here is a sample disclosure script:

Mr. Schmidt, if you have a moment right now, I was wondering if we could meet for a few minutes? (Assuming he says yes.) Thank you. You have raised an issue about my performance that I wanted to clarify in private with you.

Mr. Schmidt, I want you to know that I have an intense desire to perform at my very best level at this job; I've always had that desire from the first day I came to work at XYZ company. But Mr. Schmidt, a lot of the situations that I have been faced with so far have been very difficult for me. I have to be honest with you; multitasking is not one of my strengths. But I am very good at concentrating. In fact, I consider my focus and concentration to be among my best assets. If you ask me to work on one big project, I promise you that I will put my heart and soul into my work and you'll get fantastic results. However, I admittedly have a hard time simultaneously working on many small projects. With that said, is there any way we can adjust the kind of work I am doing to support my strengths rather than my weaknesses?

Your script doesn't have to sound at all like mine. I'm just providing a template for you. The point here is noteworthy: healthy compensation allows you to reduce your anxiety levels greatly. It allows you to focus on your strengths while not being ashamed or limited by your weaknesses. It actually helps you become your own best advocate, because you can put yourself in situations where success is possible. In other words, healthy compensation plays to your strengths and releases you from guilt for possessing certain weaknesses inherent in your neurology.

Notice that in the aforementioned disclosure script, I didn't even include the word Asperger's. In this case, it simply is not a necessary piece of information to disclose. Disclosure can sometimes make matters more complicated than they need to be.

If you used a disclosure script as I'm suggesting, you wouldn't be making any excuses to your boss. You would simply be letting your employer know the types of situations at which you will perform optimally. In essence, you're doing him a favor. If the boss reacts negatively to this disclosure statement—as some may—it is more of a reflection of him than of you.

Let's shift gears and talk about another kind of compensation—the unhealthy kind. Unhealthy compensation (also known as overcompensation) takes place unconsciously to reduce feelings of powerlessness and anxiety, but the strategy usually backfires. I'm sure you've heard of the terms "inferiority complex" or "Napoleon complex" that basically describe this concept. The physically small Napoleon established his dominance to cover up for his major insecurity of being a short man. Similarly, small dogs tend to be more aggressive and "noisy" than many big dogs, possibly due to their small size. Their behavior makes them feel bigger and less vulnerable.

Along those lines, I've heard many stories about children with Asperger's who routinely try to overcompensate for their feelings of inferiority by acting like prima donnas. For example, they snub other children who aren't as good as them at math or history. More than once, I've heard stories of Asperger's children saying "I don't want to do group work with Michael because he's stupid. He can't do math, and I could do it much better on my own." While it may be true that the Asperger's child could do math more efficiently on her own, I believe it's not the child's greatest concern. Rather, the child wants others to know that she is "good" at something, so she tries to compensate for her feelings of inferiority that stem from her unconventional social skills by acting better than others when it comes to math skills. There's nothing wrong with striving for excellence in a given area, but it should be for the right reasons. If the child is merely using math prowess as a buffer to counteract her feelings of inferiority related to the Asperger's, this would be an ill-advised strategy for increasing self-esteem.

The reason overcompensation usually backfires is because it doesn't strengthen the person's social skills or eliminate the low self-esteem generated by this area of weakness. Rather, the individual will continue to regard the lack of social skills as something that needs to be hidden because it reflects a weakness. When you accept yourself for who you are, there is no need to overcompensate.

The difference between overcompensation and healthy compensation is that when you overcompensate, you do so to cover up rather than eliminate feelings of inferiority. When you make a conscious and purposeful choice to compensate one area of weakness for an area of strength, you do so to improve your self-esteem, rather than to reduce the inferiority. By accepting yourself, warts and all, you will be able to compensate in the healthiest way possible. In doing so, you won't be continually giving away your power to other people because you will no longer see yourself as being inferior to them. Perhaps different, but not inferior.

I believe the issue of overcompensation is huge for the Asperger population because so many of us carry around feelings of inferiority. As a result, we try to make up for it in other areas. For example, unconsciously trying to succeed in business to cover up for feeling socially inept isn't a healthy way to gain self-acceptance. Being successful in business won't ultimately change the psychological issues that exist, and you'll still feel socially challenged. However, if you can fully accept your "Aspieness" and embrace both your gifts as well as your social limitations, you can then strive for excellence using your strengths rather than covering up your weaknesses.

There is a profound Zen-like paradox here: When you purposefully try to ward off feelings of powerlessness in an attempt to reduce anxiety, you will continue to feel more powerless and thus, more anxious. When you try to better yourself without trying to become more powerful and less vulnerable, you will naturally become more powerful and less vulnerable.

Perceived demands and ability to cope

There is another definition of psychological stress worth considering. It says psychological stress occurs when the demands imposed on you from the outside world outweigh your ability to cope with those demands (Evans, Marks, Murray, Skyes, Willig and Woodall 2005; Gregson and Looker 1997). Put more simply, stress results when you are overwhelmed. When there are a lot of demands on you and you have neither the stamina nor the resources to cope with those demands, stress can kick in. Those individuals with greater coping skills will be able to tolerate more stress and frustration for what the world throws at them. People without sufficient coping skills will fall victim to life's circumstances.

As I explained in *Asperger's Syndrome and Bullying* (Dubin 2007), I strongly believe people with Asperger's have relatively fewer coping skills than the neurotypical population. I will discuss why this is so in much more detail in the next chapter, but for now, let me put forth two reasons to substantiate why people with Asperger's have weak coping skills:

1. We (people with Asperger's) are not inherently good at managing the nuances of our emotions. Because we are less in control of our emotions, we are more likely to experience them on a larger scale. When they run rampant, our stress levels rise.

2. We are not inherently good at managing the details of our lives and are weak in our multitasking and organizational skills. As a result, we tend to feel under pressure when we are required to complete many different tasks simultaneously. Life circumstances—work and other activities—constantly force us to engage in multitasking activities, more frequently challenging our ability to cope. People with Asperger's have many strengths and gifts, but in general, coping with stress is not one of those gifts. If coping with the relatively uncomplicated and mundane aspects of life poses challenges for most of us with Asperger's, a real crisis will cause a magnified amount of stress that can lead to an emotional meltdown. For example, if a person with Asperger's felt great stress because he wasn't able to watch a long-awaited, favorite television program due to a power failure, it's understandable how a real crisis could totally overwhelm that person.

When confronted with circumstances you know you are not equipped to handle, life feels unfair. Imagine a mother who is trying to teach her five-year-old child how to read for the first time. It would be ridiculous if the mother asked little Johnny to read this made-up sentence, "The antidis-establishmentarianism Presbyterians interpolated their sonorous philosophy." She might as well attempt to teach Johnny calculus or put Johnny behind the wheel of a car and expect him to be able to drive without any further instructions. As human beings, we intuitively recognize these demands are unrealistic for Johnny because he has neither the skills nor resources to accomplish such impossible developmental feats. It would cause him undue frustration and stress and would lead to him to believe he can never successfully accomplish the goals expected of him. Johnny might come to believe the authority figures in his life (e.g. parents, teachers, etc.) were unfair, giving him challenges in which he was doomed to fail because he lacked the basic skills for success. Isn't that a normal human response when life's circumstances overwhelm us with more than we can handle? We then come to believe no matter how hard we try, we never have a real chance to succeed. Ultimately, we expect we will fail at the tasks others expect us to accomplish.

From the previous example, if the mother were more sensitive to her child's abilities, she would provide reading material with vocabulary words more appropriate to Johnny's age and developmental abilities. If she was a skilled teacher, she might teach words just slightly beyond Johnny's reading ability and gently guide him to phonetically sound out the new words. She may even give him subtle hints and clues but would leave it up to Johnny to decode the words. This technique is called scaffolding (Gregory, O'Neill and Soderman 2004), and educators frequently use it with students with good results. There is a logical reason why using this technique with children tends to work; it provides an appropriate amount of stress for the child to cope with in the learning process. The child has to make a potentially stressful discovery on his own, however, the educator purposefully ensures the discovery is within the child's developmental reach. Educators have learned maximum student achievement occurs when the child experiences just the right amount of stress to encourage learning a new task. Too little stress can cause a lack of motivation and too much stress can lead to disengagement. If the stress is too great, the student may become overwhelmed and experience a meltdown.

In a perfect world, teachers would provide all their students with just the right amount of scaffolding (and stress) to promote learning. No demand for performance would be completely beyond the students' ability to cope, and students would positively confront the situation at hand. This scenario generates just enough stress to fuel learning and raise the level of performance without undermining students' coping abilities. But we know the world is not always a fair place, and a person with Asperger's may often feel metaphorically challenged to learn calculus when she's only ready for pre-algebra.

People need to encounter some stress to challenge themselves to learn new skills and live productive lives. The adage, "no pain, no gain", holds an element of truth. If you are able to push yourself slightly beyond your capabilities, you'll end up increasing your skills time and again. On the other hand, if your life was stress-free and you weren't challenged to achieve new goals, the result would be a boring and stagnant journey. You would have no goals or reasons to accomplishing anything.

Think of good stress as a scaffolding situation, taking you beyond your present coping abilities. Each time you rise to the occasion in a given situation, you climb a metaphoric step on the ladder of developing successful stress management skills. With each step, you develop more frustration tolerance. For example, my first public presentation was in front of 30 people—a big challenge for me at the time. Speaking to a group this size was very stressful because I had never done it before. After I successfully accomplished that feat, I was ready to speak in front of 50 people. Then 70, 100, 200 and so on. I purposefully chose a situation to challenge myself that wouldn't be too overwhelming. It led me to take on a greater challenge the next time. My first speech was an example of good stress causing me to develop my public speaking skills. Had my first appearance been on the *Oprah Winfrey Show*, I wouldn't have had the oratory skills, the psychological backbone, or the expertise to have believed I could be successful. That challenge would have constituted bad stress.

Learn to appreciate when you are able to cope with a situation that previously would have been more than you could handle. Appreciate when you rise to the occasion and complete a task you felt was beyond your abilities. Be conscious of and celebrate your personal, professional, emotional and spiritual growth.

Finding outlets for stress, sublimation, and addictions

The hunter-gatherer societies actually had an advantage over us when it came to managing their stress (Hallowell 1997). Back then, they weren't worried about whether or not they were going to have 30 emails in their inbox when they woke up in the morning. Their fears were justifiably a lot more terrifying. At any moment, they could face imminent physical danger. As a result, they constantly had to be ready to react within their environment in a physical way. If a wild animal was on the attack, there wasn't much time to think about it or be stressed. They had to act quickly, and fortunately, they did. Thankfully, most of us do not face the day-to-day physical dangers of our hunter-gatherer ancestors, but we face other stressors we are probably not as equipped to deal with from a biological standpoint.

From an evolutionary point of view, we have retained many of the coping skills of our hunter-gatherer ancestors. We inherited from our primitive ancestors the ability to guard against external dangers. The hunter-gatherers inherited these instincts from other mammals. The mammals inherited their instincts from our cold-blooded friends, the reptiles. In fact, we have structures within our brains that serve the exact same functions as that of a snake or a rat. More on that later.

The famous cognitive therapist Aaron Beck (Hallowell 1997) was known for making the observation that we often act like hunter-gatherers when dealing with fairly trivial problems. We inherited from our ancestors a primitive way of dealing with the environment. Our nervous systems automatically shift into a "fight-or-flight" mode when we perceive a dangerous situation, just as our ancestors had to survive in the face of a saber-toothed tiger. If we did not have the ability to spring into action in life or death situations, we would have become extinct. However, there are times when this primitive response is not only maladaptive but downright dangerous.

Patsy is a woman with Asperger syndrome. She is an interior designer in her mid-thirties and always complains about being stressed. At work, when someone calls her name unexpectedly, she jumps up and her heart starts beating a mile a minute. When the telephone rings at home, she has a similar reaction. In fact, it seems as if Patsy is startled by even the smallest unexpected distraction. She has the hunter-gatherer reflex, and it has become a problem for her. Patsy rarely exercises. She complains that her stress and anxiety feel "bottled up" inside of her, with no place to go. Because her stress has no place to go, the energy from her anxiety fuels her stress.

Sound familiar? Many people with Asperger's startle easily. An unexpected stimulus, such as someone casually calling out their name, can create that discomfort. The fight-or-flight response then begins pumping all kinds of chemicals, such as cortisol, into our nervous systems to get us ready for battle. But sometimes there is no battle. Many people today—not just those with Asperger's—physiologically react to stress as if they are preparing to run away from that proverbial saber-toothed tiger, even when the tiger doesn't exist. Either the car broke down, or an Internet glitch on the computer can trigger an extreme stress response.

The human response to stress is something we inherited from our ancestors. This response served a purpose and still does in some circumstances, but not in others. We all have the instinct to run away from the ancestral saber-toothed tiger, but when we want to run away from a boss who is merely summoning us, we need to find constructive, substitute outlets for our stress that don't warrant a fight-or-flight response. Sometimes, these outlets can become dangerous. Addictions develop when the outlets for stress or depression cover up the unwanted negative feelings as opposed to truly transforming them. When life gets too overwhelming for some people, addictions are an attempt to chase away the blues and anxiety. When a depressed person turns to alcohol, drugs, or gambling, or an anxious person becomes addicted to tranquilizers, they do so as an outlet for their stress or depression, believing these outlets will make their problems and the resulting stress go away. Unfortunately, these ill-chosen outlets only create additional problems that compromise the individual's mental and physical health.

On the other hand, those people who exercise, meditate, and engage in activities that stimulate their minds are finding appropriate outlets through sublimating the instinct to run away from that saber-toothed tiger.

Sublimation is one of Sigmund Freud's (Kahn 2002) classic defense mechanisms everyone employs. Many psychologists view it as one of the few defense mechanisms that can create positive results. Other defense mechanisms such as projection and repression are almost always unhealthy. Sublimation, on the other hand, can be very healthy. Sublimation simply means channeling one form of desire into a more constructive activity. Exercise is a form of sublimation in which you are releasing bodily tensions that you might use in an aggressive manner. Great artists sublimate all the time. Suppose an artist had a sexual fettish he wanted to act out, but chose not to because societal norms classified the fetish as taboo or even criminal. Now suppose he channeled the libidinal energies from his fantasies into creating beautiful, erotic artwork—something society would accept and view as beneficial. This is sublimation. A more simplistic example of sublimation is if I were angry about something my boss had done, instead of following my impulse to punch him, I may go home and hit my punching bag for 45 minutes. I would still be relieving my need to hit something, but it wouldn't be my boss. Because of my sublimation, I would keep my job.

Sublimation doesn't always produce a great result. According to Harry Stack Sullivan (Evans 1996), the founder of interpersonal psychoanalysis, human beings sometimes sublimate certain unacceptable drives with other ones. Here's an example:

> Joe is a neurotypical accountant who happens to be very shy. He has consistently turned down invitations to company parties and other social events because he feels discomfort when he believes others perceive him as being shy or socially awkward. However, he understands that to move up at his accounting firm, he has to become more socially active. Joe has become very anxious about his job security unless he extends himself beyond his comfort zone. So he decides to try having a glass or two of alcohol before attending his first party. To his utter joy, he was like a different person at the party. He felt alive and spontaneous, finally able to connect with the other guests. Joe then develops a new pattern in his life. Anytime before he has to socialize, he has a few drinks. He sees the alcohol as his lifeline. Since he has to socialize regularly, he starts drinking regularly. Eventually, he develops a drinking problem.

What was Joe's natural desire? To get away from all social encounters due to his anxiety. Because social inhibition isn't an acceptable trait for job advancement, Joe sublimated his urge to not socialize with his willingness to be more social as long as he could use alcohol to facilitate the transition into the social situation. Once he saw social isolation was not a viable option, he turned to alcohol to cover up his isolationism. The alcohol gave him instant comfort in social situations. Joe eventually replaced his original behavior, the tendency to isolate himself from other people, with another unhealthy behavior: to become a compulsive drinker. Did Joe want to become a compulsive drinker? Was that his original intent? Of course not. As Sullivan says, the sublimated behavior isn't always what we want for ourselves, but is an unintended byproduct of wanting to change our behavior.

When you sublimate your desires properly, you do so not to cover up one bad action with another bad action or one bad feeling with another bad feeling, but to replace an unhealthy desire with a more constructive one.

Life in the 21st century challenges us to sublimate our primitive reactions to stress in healthy ways. Think about all the stresses you face daily. Some common stressors among adults are:

1. Emails to check on and respond to on a daily basis.

2. Responsibilities at work.

3. Bills to pay.

4. Errands to run.

5. Life survival activities, e.g. preparing meals, maintaining a house and car.

From that list, did you notice how much multitasking is involved in our lives? Aside from the fact that paying bills is inherently unpleasant and possibly stressful and that car repairs are inherently annoying, multitasking is a skill that does not come naturally to those of us with Asperger's. For us, it's a double whammy. Not only do we have to multitask, we have to multitask while accomplishing tasks that will sometimes be stressful or annoying.

This takes us full circle and back to the saber-toothed tiger. Our reactions to these demands are compounded by the fact that we have so many of them to deal with, producing a physiological response comparable to running away from a saber-toothed tiger. Because of this genetically determined response, you may end up dealing with these reactions in very unproductive or unhealthy ways, as previously discussed. Over time, the health consequences of having such reactions can be disastrous for numerous reasons. This book will discuss ways to change your hunter-gatherer reactions to stress into healthy reactions that are more appropriate for living a healthy and successful life.

Applying the brakes

Think of your body as an automobile. When there is a need to accelerate, you simply put your foot on the gas pedal. When there is a need to slow down, you put your foot on the brake pedal. The body operates in a similar way through the sympathetic and parasympathetic nervous systems, which are part of the autonomic nervous system. This system makes us stop and go like an automobile.

According to author Robert Sapolsky (1994) from his witty book, *Why Zebras Don't Get Ulcers*, the job of the sympathetic nervous system is to spring you into action when there is an impending stressor or emergency. Sapolsky describes the sympathetic nervous system as mediating the four f's of behavior: flight, fight, fright and sex. (That's his joke, not mine.)

When you become alarmed or frightened, your sympathetic nervous system mobilizes you into battle. The sympathetic nervous system releases epinephrine [adrenaline] and norepinephrine [noradrenaline] (norepinephrine is synthesized by dopamine) throughout the body almost instantly upon feeling stressed. Your heartbeat immediately begins increasing and your digestive organs shut down and begin conserving energy. Your cognition sharpens and you temporarily feel more alert. Blood rushes from your internal organs to your outer muscles where the energy is most needed. Cortisol is quickly secreted, serving to minimize physical pain, give you a quick boost of energy, and temporarily sharpen your memory. In essence, the sympathetic nervous system is the system that helps you flee from that proverbial saber-toothed tiger.

At some point, you need to put your foot on the brake pedal to slow down the sympathetic nervous system from making your body work overtime. That's when the parasympathetic nervous system comes into play. The parasympathetic nervous system helps you conserve energy during periods of non-stress. It draws blood back to the organs, aids in digestion and slows down the beating of your heart after the stressor has passed. It relaxes you and allows you to experience some sense of relief. While both the sympathetic and parasympathetic nervous systems are always active within you, one system is usually dominant at any one time because the parts of your brain that activate one nervous system will automatically inhibit the other.

What happens when the parasympathetic nervous system isn't functioning properly and doesn't turn "on" over a long period of time? Bad things happen. Because your brain cannot activate both systems at once, it becomes accustomed to just keeping the sympathetic nervous system on, even when there's no stressors confronting you. (Sapolsky 1994). According to Sapolsky, if you are constantly turning on your sympathetic nervous system, you are chronically shutting off the parasympathetic nervous system. This explains why you sometimes feel prolonged anxiety and unable to feel safe and relaxed, even after the stressor has passed.

Let's put this within an Asperger's framework. In the general literature on Asperger's, researchers agree anxiety is a major issue for our population (Attwood 2006; Gaus 2007; Ghaziuddin 2005; Klin, Sparrow and Volkmar 2000). Much has been written in the general literature about the problems we have when it comes to "shifting gears" and transitioning between one activity and another or from one emotional state to another. Perhaps inherently, we simply have a harder time "putting on the brakes". Our sympathetic nervous systems may be on overdrive much of the time. If this is the case, it means we have to work extra hard to shift gears between excitatory and relaxation states because it may not come as naturally and easily to us as it does to others. Some people recover relatively quickly after they have just experienced a stressful event or occurrence. If that doesn't describe you, don't worry. The ensuing chapters will teach you strategies for putting on the brakes.

Daryl is a young man in his mid-twenties diagnosed with Asperger syndrome. Today, Daryl has a meeting with his boss over a very important matter. Daryl realizes this meeting may determine his place within the company's pecking order and has spent the previous night gearing up for it. By the time he walks into his boss's office, his sympathetic nervous system has kicked in full throttle. His heart is beating fast, his cognition is sharp and he feels fresh and alert as ever. As it turns out, Daryl and his boss have an excellent meeting.

Daryl is relieved now, but he doesn't feel at peace. Even though the meeting is over, he feels his heart still racing; he sees his face is still flushed and his stomach is in knots. "Something is not right," Daryl thinks to himself. "The meeting is over, it went well, and yet I'm not relaxed yet. What is going on?"

This is a case of someone's parasympathetic nervous system not kicking in at the appropriate time. As someone with Asperger's, Daryl has a hard time shifting gears from one activity to another, especially an activity that has some importance attached to it. This results in Daryl having a hard time applying the brakes after his interview. Because Daryl has not trained himself to relax after stressful situations, his parasympathetic nervous system has not learned how it is supposed to function. As a result, Daryl feels stressed all the time.

The sympathetic and parasympathetic nervous systems oscillating back and forth are as natural as a person inhaling oxygen and exhaling carbon dioxide. Yet one can only imagine how tough it would be to do hold your breath without exhaling. Well, never "applying the breaks" is virtually the same thing as forgetting to exhale. Let me use myself as an example to illustrate this point more clearly.

When I was a teenager, I was an extremely competitive tennis player, primarily due to years of training with a professional tennis coach who put a lot of pressure on me to win my matches. Before an important match, I used to get myself all juiced up. I would put on my walkman and listen to energizing music that would get the adrenaline flowing throughout my body. By the time I stepped on to the court, I was like a virtual energizer bunny. My sympathetic nervous system was approaching overdrive.

After the match was over, whether I won or lost, I had a hard time coming down from the excitement of the match. I would replay certain points in my head repeatedly and relive those points as if they were happening for the first time. If I won the match, I basked in the glory of triumph and reveled as the victor. If I lost, I dwelled on the defeat and thought about what I could have done differently. Either way, I never could relax after the match. If I had to play another match the next day, I sometimes felt too tired because my parasympathetic nervous system did not kick in after the first match was over and allow me to conserve energy and relax. My energy tank was often running on empty. My sympathetic nervous system was still in charge.

This often happens to me, even to this day, when I make an important presentation in front of hundreds of people. I'll notice I have a hard time coming down or relaxing. I even experience this sensation following routine meetings I have with my doctoral faculty supervisor. It is frustrating when I just can't seem to relax after the stressful event has passed. What I believe is happening is that I simply have a hard time shifting emotional gears and thus, I have a hard time shifting physiological gears. My sympathetic nervous system dominates my parasympathetic nervous system. Do I think this has something to do with my Asperger syndrome? You bet I do.

But there is another reason why learning how to apply the brakes is crucially important for your health. If your sympathetic nervous system doesn't allow the parasympathetic nervous system to kick in, your body is working overtime. You will be more at risk for heart disease, poor memory (Punset 2007), decreased immune performance, and type II diabetes, as well as a host of other issues. Because your health is at stake, you *must* learn how to apply the brakes.

But that's not the end of the story. Let us now study the organ most involved with the stress response—the brain.

Emotional hijackings

In the 1970s, researcher Paul MacLean proposed an elegant model of the brain called the Triune Brain Model (Cozolino 2002). In part, this model helped to reconcile both Charles Darwin's theory of evolution and Sigmund Freud's model of the mind; both being models that claimed human beings had a rather primitive side to them. Darwin felt that human beings were driven toward survival and competition, while Freud concurred humans are, at least in part, driven by this impersonal, animalistic force called the id. The Triune brain model helped to make sense of these theories.

To put this in layman's terms, our brains contain structures that keep us connected to our evolutionary past. This means we share some basic instincts with reptiles as well as rats and all other mammals.

The primitive part of the brain is aptly labeled the reptilian brain or R-complex. We have this part of the brain we have in common with reptiles. It includes the cerebellum and the brain stem.

Higher on the evolutionary ladder is the limbic system or the "emotional brain", which we share with mammals. This part of the brain is also called the paleomammalian brain. As you would probably expect, the limbic system is more complicated than the R-complex. This part of the brain is responsible for more complex emotions along with the consolidation of long-term memory.

Lastly, there is the neocortex (or new cortex), which is the most recently evolved part of the brain. This part of the brain is responsible for higher-order thinking, abstraction, and advanced cognition. It is known as the "thinking" brain.

In a stressful situation, the neocortex has the least amount of influence over the actions you will end up performing. Think about what that means. When you are stressed, the R-complex and the limbic system override the rational part of your brain. When you are stressed, you might behave like a snake or a rat because you have inherited from them the same self-protective mechanisms. Have you ever noticed sometimes you don't act like yourself when you're under too much stress? For example, you've had a bad day, and at the end of it, someone comes up to you and makes a snide remark. Without even stopping to think, you retort back with a snide or angry comment of your own. Had you had the necessary time to think about it, your neocortex might have asserted itself and you might have thought, "Hey man, just ignore this guy. He's a real punk and is harmless. Just walk away and smile." But you've had a hard day and your sympathetic nervous system has worked overtime. Because you are stressed out, the animalistic part of your psyche takes control and hijacks any rational response that would have been appropriate for this situation.

You might think the word "hijack" is too strong a word for what I am describing. In fact, that's exactly what is happening. According to Daniel Goleman (1995), author of *Emotional Intelligence,* emotional hijackings take place all the time. The limbic system is usually involved to a great degree in these hijackings, which sabotage your rational judgment under moments of duress.

The amygdala (Goleman 1995) is a part of the limbic system and is known as "the seat of all passion". In essence, you can think of the amygdala as the first-alert warning system of your brain. Your amygdala is connected via the hypothalamus to the sympathetic nervous system, which in turn signals for the fight-or-flight reaction, even before the thinking brain has had a chance to process the situation (O'Connor 2005). That is why you move out of the way as the bus is approaching, before you even have a chance to realize what's happening. It is also why you pull your hand away from the stove before you consciously register the thought "Wow, that's hot."

The amygdala scans the environment, constantly detecting threats. Once it detects a threat, its voice booms 10,000 times louder than that of the neocortex. It proceeds to override your higher-order thinking to protect you when it senses you are in danger. According to Goleman, many people, when emotionally hijacked by stress, later wonder what came over them after the stressor has passed. Often times, they can't even believe that they acted in such an irrational way.

What's more, research tells us that if the amygdala hijacks you enough times, new connections form between the neurons in the amygdala (O'Connor 2005) and you become more anxious in general. For example, if you are fearful of meeting strangers and you are in a position where you have to meet strangers frequently, O'Conner says that eventually, you may become worried about other things besides meeting new people. Your amygdala is gaining strength via these new connections. O'Connor hypothesizes this is how repeated, specific fears can turn into free-floating anxiety. Don't worry, it's not all that complicated. The message here is: the more you worry, the more you'll worry.

Panic attacks

Sometimes anxiety seems to come completely out of nowhere. It seems to be free-floating. Like an earthquake, no warning precipitates the intense wave of anxiety that hits you out of nowhere.

Living through a full-fledged panic attack (Bourne 2005) can be a frightening experience. In a panic attack, the fight-or-flight reaction takes over without an apparent trigger. This might be the equivalent of how it would feel to have *alien hand syndrome,* which is when the hand behaves in a manner that is totally contradictory to the body's wishes (Carter 2000). Due to various injuries to different parts of the brain, the alien hand can actually cause you to accomplish the exact opposite of what you want your hand to do. Carter (2000) gives an example of a man who, with his right hand, went to grab a piece of clothing from his wardrobe only to have his alien left hand grab something else. With alien hand syndrome, you feel as if an entirely different person is controlling your hand. To paraphrase the cognitive therapist, Aaron Beck (1985), a panic attack is described as a slippage of one's ability to control things. You lose control over your ability to stay calm and emotionally centered.

During a panic attack, your sympathetic nervous system acts like the alien hand. It springs into action without your consent. Like the sufferer with the alien hand, your body seems to have a mind of its own. It feels as if a demonic entity has taken possession of you even though that is not what is actually happening. Since your body behaves so unpredictably during a panic attack, you might even feel like you are having a heart attack or are in the process of dying. Believe me, if you've had a panic attack before, there is no mistaking it for anything else. It is very frightening and often takes a significant amount of time to recover.

Traumatic stress

Most human beings experience episodes in their lives that are of a traumatic nature. However, among the many traumatic experiences people with Asperger's can encounter, the one that seems to be most common is to be the victim of childhood bullying (Attwood 2006). The wounds you may be carrying from being bullied are of a devastating nature and probably influence how you interact with others. Research tells us those chronically bullied as children have a difficult time with things such as dating and forming relationships (Gilmartin 1987). However, it doesn't end there. If you have a developmental "disability" or difference (as I like to call it) such as Asperger's, the odds dramatically increase that you probably experienced severe traumatic stress as a child. Here are a couple of sobering statistics:

1. A person with a developmental disability is two to ten times more likely to have experienced sexual abuse (Westat Inc 1993).

2. Most of the sexual abuse that takes place is committed by immediate family members and can also include acts of physical

abuse, neglect and emotional abuse (Knutson and Sullivan 2000).

If you were the victim of this kind of inexcusable, indefensible, and barbaric abuse, your pain probably goes deeper than words can express. You may even have a condition called post-traumatic stress disorder (PTSD). PTSD is a severe anxiety disorder that can develop as a result of being exposed to a terrible past event, such as being the victim of severe abuse. For example, as an adult, if you see someone who even slightly reminds you of your childhood perpetrator, it can trigger a full-fledged panic attack.

Psychologist and Asperger's expert, Dr. Tony Attwood (2006) says the clinical signs of PTSD include attempts to avoid the triggers that remind you of the person or incident that traumatized you, signs of intense anxiety, depression, and even intense anger. Attwood (2006) notes that for people with Asperger's, being the victim of bullying in childhood is a common precipitator toward developing PTSD later in life. He recommends the use of cognitive-behavioral therapy (CBT) to treat PTSD. An entire chapter on CBT follows.

Now that we have explored the nature of stress, it's time to hone in on the experience of having Asperger's and how it contributes to the anxiety we experience in our daily lives. First, though, I suggest reviewing the list of action points from this chapter.

Action points

- Bear in mind that one form of psychological stress happens when you feel vulnerable when confronted by a source of power.

- Do not ascribe power to people and situations that actually are not, in reality, worthy of that kind of power.

- Consciously use healthy compensation to reduce anxiety levels. Feeling inferior is not a reason to compensate.

- Accept yourself for who you are and there is no need to overcompensate.

- True growth occurs when you put yourself in situations that are slightly beyond your comfort zone, creating slight stress. Try to challenge yourself!

- Find appropriate outlets for your stress without falling into the trap of developing unhealthy addictions.

- The parasympathetic nervous system's job is to help you relax. Learn to let it do its job.

- Be careful the animalistic parts of your brain don't make you more anxious than you need to be.

Asperger syndrome and anxiety

Neurotypical people often ask me to describe what living with Asperger syndrome is like. Since I consider those who are diagnosed with Asperger's to be the greatest experts (and teachers) in describing the experience of having Asperger's, I believe you and I know more than a lot of the so called "experts". For example, some neurotypicals have stated that people with Asperger's are not capable of empathy. I disagree. That is why I want to devote a chapter to describing what living with Asperger's is like. You may laugh, cry, or even scream, but I hope I validate many of the feelings you have experienced in your life. That is my goal in writing this chapter.

Stranger in a strange land

Ever since you were a child, you have been conditioned to fit into a certain kind of mold—that proverbial square peg into the round hole. You've been told your eccentricities were bad, that your special interests were weird, that your nonconformist behaviors were problematic, and if you only tried harder, you would do better. You have probably viewed yourself as being defective, weird, nerdy, and some other negative adjectives. You have most likely viewed others as powerful and yourself as powerless. As you grew up, your self-image eventually coalesced around the opinions of others and you eventually internalized those opinions. "I am that geeky, lonely, eccentric, nonconformist troublemaker with poor social skills."

What I'm going to do throughout this book is shift your perception of yourself into something that's a lot more realistic and accurate.

It won't be easy because old patterns are always hard to break, but I also know change is possible if we truly desire it. We'll work at change together.

An acquired skill

Let me ask you to accept a simple truth: you will probably have to work much harder at managing your stress than most neurotypicals. It just doesn't come as naturally to us as it does to them. I wish I could tell you otherwise, but I wouldn't be truthful. For us, learning stress management is much more of an acquired skill than an inherited talent. If you can't accept this truth, life is going to be a constant struggle for you. You'll always be wishing life was easier and if only you didn't have Asperger syndrome, your life would be better. Once you affirm the reality that you may have to work harder than most neurotypicals to control your stress, you will come to see yourself in a new light—as a warrior, someone with a level of bravery that rivals a soldier heading into a battle. I'm not saying this to boost your ego. I'm being honest with you. The bravery and courage it takes to live as a person with Asperger's in a neurotypical world is astounding, and yet you do it every single day. Give yourself credit for exhibiting that strength.

Converting anxiety into bravery

How do you change your mindset from that of a fearful person to a brave warrior who resiliently meets life with conviction? It can be done, but not without confronting certain obstacles. For example, I've met dozens of people with Asperger's who were wrongly discriminated against at their jobs and fired without cause, despite laws to prevent this type of unfairness from happening. I've met children with Asperger's in the public schools who are constantly underserved. Their teachers don't understand their behavior, nor are they aware of ways to teach them in the most effective manner. These children are often mislabeled as emotionally disturbed, and they're bullied by their peers without recourse. Is it any wonder that we become anxious as adults?

The truth is, you can shake your fist at the world all you want, but the alchemical work of turning "lead into gold" has to begin with you. All transformation begins from within you. The process of learning how to convert anxiety into true bravery doesn't happen by trying to change the world. You must assume primary responsibility for setting your own agenda, taking the necessary action, and not falling victim to your own internal processes and anxiety. If you use others' unfair treatment of you (because of your Asperger's) as an excuse for continuing to be anxious, you will let others always get the better of you. This is hardly a warrior's mentality. Therefore, you must work on developing more effective ways of managing your anxiety, recognizing it's probably going to be more challenging for you than most people, and recognizing the world is not always going to be a fair place, especially toward people with Asperger's and other disabilities. No one said this process was going to be easy, but as I have said, it is doable.

There are a myriad of reasons to explain why individuals with Asperger's experience greater amounts of stress, and we will continue to explore the major ones in the ensuing chapters. In this chapter, however, I'd like to examine some of the characteristics of Asperger's along with a few coexisting conditions and observe how these character traits contribute to higher stress levels. In my previous book, I listed multiple reasons why I felt people with Asperger's were vulnerable to bullies. I believe many of the same reasons I listed in that book are applicable to our discussion on why we experience stress. Let's look at a few of the most pertinent reasons.

Low frustration tolerance

Hypersensitivities

Many of us with Asperger syndrome have a low tolerance for dealing with frustrating situations and events in our lives. There are many reasons why this is so. Did you ever notice you just can't stand being under fluorescent lights? Maybe the humming of the lights bothers you or perhaps it's the unnatural color spectrum. Perhaps you are bothered when you are around certain smells. They drive you absolutely bonkers. I've met some people with Asperger's who must leave a room if they happen to dislike the smell in the room. These responses are called hypersensitivities and they are very common for our population. Hypersensitivities happen when one of your five senses overloads with too much input. For people with Asperger's and other autism spectrum disorders (ASD), one or more of our five senses are often extremely sensitive and can get easily overloaded (Attwood 2006). You may be less tolerant than most people are of bright lights, loud noises, certain kinds of fabrics, etc. These hypersensitivities can cause undue stress in your life. If fluorescent lights bother you, then certain office or work environments may be problematic. If various smells bother you, it means you probably have to be careful in choosing the cafeteria settings or restaurants that are acceptable for you to frequent. If loud noises bother you, it means that most parties and celebratory occasions will be stressful instead of fun. Perhaps a story will put this in perspective:

Will is a young man with an undiagnosed case of Asperger syndrome. He and his wife are still asleep. It's 6:00 a.m. and the alarm clock goes off. The abrasive noise of the alarm jolts Will out of bed, but his wife wakes up gracefully. He's always hated that noise and his wife can't understand why. "It's just a normal alarm," she says. "If it was quieter, we wouldn't hear it, and we would remain asleep." They've had constant arguments about getting a clock with a less intrusive alarm, but so far, Will has lost those arguments.

Now Will is off to work. He lives in the heart of Manhattan, a bustling city with a lot of commotion and chaos. As Will steps outside to greet the day, he encounters taxis honking, strong smells from the deli next door, and an ambulance passing with a blaring siren. Within a few minutes, he feels a headache coming over him. "This happens every single day," he thinks to himself. "I always get these headaches right after leaving the house. What's going on?"

Will arrives at work, but he smells the coffee that his co-workers are drinking and starts to feel queasy. The smell of coffee makes Will sick to his stomach. He immediately goes outside and waits to come back to his cubicle until he is sure that the co-workers won't be in the vicinity.

Perfectionism

If you're a black-and-white thinker (and people with Asperger's tend to exhibit rigidity in their thinking), it's possible that you have developed a very narrow definition of success. Unless you are 100 per cent successful at an endeavor, you may consider your attempt a complete failure. People with Asperger's have very low frustration tolerance when they are unable to be completely successful in their goal-oriented activities. I've met children with Asperger's who, when getting 98 per cent on a test, cry because it wasn't 100 per cent. People with Asperger's have impending fears of failure. It's logical if you stop to think about it. Since many aspects of life do not come naturally to you, it would make sense you would be anxious about the pursuit of goals in areas where you also may possess some weakness. It would also make sense you would be inclined to try harder because things like socializing and multitasking are inherently more challenging for you. If a person with Asperger syndrome is reprimanded constantly at work, he will probably become hyper-vigilant about his job performance. If that same person continues to experience social rejection, he is going to try extra hard to win people over. If this person isn't careful, he may try to overcompensate in some other area where he is naturally strong and meets his perfectionist standards. Of course, it's impossible to achieve total perfection and thus, he will most likely continue to regard himself as a failure.

Mr. Smith is in his mid-forties and has been diagnosed with Asperger syndrome. Mr. Smith feels he cannot do anything right. At work, his boss constantly reminds him of how to make cold calls (telephone solicitations). Since Mr. Smith has been reprimanded so many times for saying the wrong things when making these cold calls, he has scripted out the calls. He practices to make sure the inflection in his voice is just the way his boss wants it. He's become obsessed with this. He practices his cold call delivery in the shower, in the car, while watching TV, even when he's on the Internet. Like Ivan Pavlov's dogs, who became conditioned to salivate upon hearing the ringing of a bell, Mr. Smith has become conditioned to feel like a failure. As a result, he works extra hard so as to not feel like a failure.

Mr. Smith becomes increasingly aware that he experiences rejection in many areas of his life. He wants to feel that he is good at something, so he begins to devote all of his energy into his childhood passion, art. Spending nights alone with his easel, Mr. Smith works tirelessly to produce something of beauty and value to the world. To compensate for his poor cold calling skills, Mr. Smith finds success in his painting.

Unpredictability

People with Asperger's have a low frustration tolerance toward unpredictability, and life is unpredictable in almost every respect. The fact that you may have a hard time dealing with life's glitches (as I like to call them) is another reason why you probably feel you have to be hyper-vigilant. Most likely, you feel like you constantly have to be on guard for things that could possibly happen around you. Will the car break down today? Will the flight be delayed? What will happen at the meeting today? Will everything go according to plan? As you can see, this kind of thinking is the perfect recipe for developing obsessive-compulsive disorder (OCD). The energy you expend detecting possible threats in the environment is depleting. It takes a lot of energy to be anxious about every possible thing that can go wrong. Later on in the book, you're going to learn how to differentiate between true threats and cognitive illusions, especially in the chapter on CBT.

Transitioning

People with Asperger's are known for having low frustration toward making smooth transitions between activities. When a situation is threatening and takes a lot of energy to confront, it makes the next situation that much more daunting. If I am relieved to have made it to work because driving is hard for me, I will have to recover from the drive before I'm able to focus on my job. All of a sudden, I realize my job is just as threatening as the drive to work and my sympathetic nervous system has not yet had a chance to slow down. If everything in life is perceived as being threatening, it's hard to find and appreciate moments of tranquility when the threats aren't present.

Monotropism

As self-advocate, Wendy Lawson, explains (2003) people with Asperger's tend to process information in bits and pieces as opposed to taking in the big picture. This is what she calls "monotropism". When a person is monotropic, it means that he or she will focus on small details and have a hard time synthesizing them into a coherent understanding of the entire situation. In the literature, this behavior is described as "poor central coherence" (Attwood 2006). A person with good central coherence understands how all the metaphoric puzzle pieces fit together without getting stuck on one or two of the pieces. He or she is able to look at the puzzle in its entirety.

Many people with Asperger's have good central coherence when it comes to understanding processes that Simon Baron-Cohen describes as "folk physics" (Baron-Cohen 1997). Someone with Asperger's might be able to explain how quantum physics, chaos theory, and other complicated scientific processes work, yet be stumped to explain basic psychological processes that most neurotypicals take for granted, such as why people act a certain way at dinner parties. What I've just described is a discrepancy in one's intelligence between how things work and how people behave. It's a discrepancy common among people with Asperger's. This lack of social understanding is what Baron-Cohen calls a deficit in folk psychology. Because "things" usually progress more consistently than people behave in most situations, in some ways, "things" are easier to understand than people are for some individuals with Asperger's. This being the case, I theorize the person with Asperger's can use his monotropism to understand the details of how "things" work, so as to eventually gain a better grasp on the entire picture. Frequently, however, many people with Asperger's are highly intuitive when it comes to folk physics and are able to see the big picture without much effort; a skill that doesn't seem to work the same way in social situations.

Monotropism in social situations

Many of us with Asperger's are so absorbed with the details of a given situation, we end up missing other important details and consequently aren't very good social problem solvers. I would venture this causes stress on a daily basis because it is harder to see social situations globally. You may only focus on one aspect of the social encounter. Again, because you have to work so hard in social situations, it's hard to know what to focus on and what to ignore. Your challenges with auditory processing may make it nearly impossible to process all incoming information, so conversation is a huge strain. You never know when to respond, what to respond to, the inflection with which you should respond, etc. You can now begin to appreciate how being monotropic in social situations creates a huge amount of anxiety for you.

> Sheila is a woman in her mid-thirties with Asperger syndrome who has been invited to a dinner party and is nervous about attending. Although she was not asked to bring something, she finds upon arriving she was the only one who didn't bring a bottle of wine or some food. "I didn't even think about that," Sheila thinks to herself. "I was so preoccupied with preparing for this party and practicing how to be a good party guest I didn't even think about bringing something. I thought if I brought something I would be the only one who did. How was I supposed to know? Now I look foolish." Sheila was so preoccupied with certain details she missed other important details. This is a classic example of monotropism, poor central coherence and a deficit in folk psychology.

When you fall victim to your own social misjudgments enough times, it begins to take on a toll on your psychological well-being. Again, like one of Pavlov's dogs, you become conditioned to feel like a social failure, thus encouraging a kind of hyper-vigilance on your part. The problem is the more hyper-vigilant you become, the more monotropic you will become. You will become so obsessed with certain details you'll likely miss other details, like Sheila not bringing something to the party. She was so pre-occupied with trying to avoid making a mistake at the party, she unwittingly committed another social faux pas.

It's likely your perceived repeated failures in social situations have encouraged you to become more monotropic in these situations so as to not make future mistakes. However, it is your monotropism that is causing you to make these social mistakes in the first place. That is the paradox. You are trying to help yourself by using a strategy that is actually backfiring every time.

What's the solution here? Whether or not you believe this, much of the problem takes place in your own head. When you begin to reframe these situations and put less pressure on yourself, you'll begin to relax. When you relax, you'll become less hyper-vigilant and, consequently, it will free up your energy. For example, Sheila was concentrating so hard on trying to be a "good party guest" she ultimately was spiting herself in the process. Had she just relaxed and let her guard down, she might have remembered to bring some food or wine to the party. Even if she had not remembered, she would not have attached so much significance to the fact that she had forgotten. She would have thought to herself, "Okay, things like this happen from time to time. I'm not going to be hard on myself. I do have Asperger's. I know what my strengths and weaknesses are. I may not be the best at making decisions in social situations, but I'm good at a lot of other things." Taking this attitude, Sheila is not viewing herself as a social failure. She's viewing herself as a human being, someone with strengths and weaknesses.

This foreshadows information you'll learn later in this book, but keep in mind a lot of the anxiety and stress you experience happens in your mind, not in the real world. When you change your thoughts to mirror reality more accurately, you'll free up energy that has been used on worrying.

One thing you may have to come to accept as a person with Asperger's is you will likely make more social faux pas than most people. The significance you attach to these perceived social mistakes will contribute directly to your level of anxiety on a daily basis. For example, before my diagnosis of Asperger's, I was always hard on myself when I made a social mistake related to my monotropism. I would scold myself; tell myself how worthless I was, and ultimately, I would become extremely anxious at the next social situation. I don't do that anymore. Instead, I try to learn from the mistake so that I can avoid making it again. My focus is on recognizing my limitations and accepting them.

If you are able to capitalize on your strengths while recognizing you may have some social limitations, you will take the pressure off yourself and free yourself from needless anxiety. You can't be perfect at everything. No one is. But you do have control over how much you browbeat yourself for making social mistakes.

Problems reading nonverbal cues

Research tells us that 85 per cent of the communication that takes place between human beings is nonverbal (Young 1998). Just imagine what that means. If people with Asperger's struggle with interpreting nonverbal cues (which we do), we are missing out on the majority of communication that is taking place. Not only does this make communication a frustrating venture, but it also causes a lot of anxiety. Since you can never be sure you are correctly interpreting someone else's body language and/or nonverbal cues, it forces you to work harder to understand what is being communicated. Since working harder takes more energy day in and day out, it can become an exhausting endeavor. The exhaustion gives way to anxiety, and it becomes a never-ending vicious circle.

> Hank is a bright, educated individual with Asperger's in his mid-thirties. He graduated high school and college with honors. On paper, Hank should be successful in the workplace and in relationships. Yet, he finds those domains of daily living challenging.

> Hank can never seem to get past a first date. Once he tried to kiss a girl when she was not ready. Another time he withheld his affection from a girl for fear of acting too soon. At work, he jabbers, totally unaware of the body language of his co-workers.

Hank is chronically anxious. He is never sure if he's reading the situation correctly. "Should I keep talking or stay silent? Should I make a move or wait a little? Am I annoying this person? I can't tell if this person is annoyed and I don't know what to do."

Perhaps you have felt a bit like Hank at times. I think we all have. It's like being a foreigner and not knowing the customs and rituals of a particular land. I have often told neurotypicals that if they want to know what having Asperger's is like, just travel to a foreign land where the language, customs, and culture are unfamiliar. Essentially, that's what life feels like for Hank and many of us with Asperger's. Since reading nonverbal cues are not Hank's strong suit, he is constantly befuddled by other people's behavior. He also wonders if his responses are appropriate. After all, if Hank doesn't understand the intention behind people's nonverbal actions, his responses may be in contrast to what is actually being communicated.

Auditory processing difficulties

Aside from the challenges people with Asperger's have reading nonverbal cues, many of us also have difficulties processing auditory information quickly. Much of the auditory information we receive gets muffled. In day-to-day conversations, we have to work harder than our neurotypical counterparts when it comes to processing incoming information. While neurotypicals naturally understand subtle vocal intonations and nuances, it may not come as easily for you and me. Consequently, we may tend to analyze what people are saying to make sure we are correctly interpreting what we are hearing. This effort to understand another person becomes tiring over a long period of time, and it is anxiety provoking.

While you may misunderstand certain vocal intonations that might connote sarcasm or irony, you understand most verbal communication. Since your auditory processing may be delayed, it takes you a little longer to be able to decode what was just said. As a consequence, you might find yourself thinking a little longer before actually responding, causing your responses to lack spontaneity and instead seem very deliberate.

If you have poor auditory processing and trouble understanding vocal intonation as far as intent is concerned, it can cause you angst in a number of casual situations. You may have a hard time telling the difference between sarcasm and seriousness. In situations where rapid-fire responses are expected, you may feel pressed for time. For example, if you are interviewing for a job and the employer is grilling you with question after question, you may feel pressured to answer every question quickly in order to get the job. But since it takes you a few seconds longer to process the information, you don't want to be too hasty and sacrifice thoughtfulness. Therefore, you're caught in a bind. "Should I respond right away so as to appear neurotypical, or wait a few seconds and give a more meaningful reply?" This is the kind of anxiety that most of us with Asperger's face on a daily basis.

If I were coaching you in this very difficult situation, I would encourage you to give meaningful answers rather than opting for expediency. If your answers are deliberate, well-informed, and logical, chances are the boss will choose you over someone who is able to reply quickly but with less substance. Wouldn't you rather have quality over quantity?

Coexisting conditions

No two people with Asperger's are the same. The Asperger's population is a diverse group of people. It's entirely possible to meet two individuals with Asperger's who have totally different temperaments, aptitudes, and social preferences (introversion, extroversion). It's likely to meet someone with Asperger's who is a computer geek and someone else with no technical prowess; someone whose main interest is science and someone else with no scientific inclinations; someone who is a star athlete and someone else with no athletic ability. While this may seem fairly obvious and trivial on the surface, it's important to keep this point in mind as it is often unnoticed. Many people assume that if a person has Asperger syndrome, it means he or she must be a mechanical engineer who has savant-like abilities. I'd like to break down that stereotype by showing that people with Asperger's come in all shapes and sizes.

This point becomes even more relevant when trying to understand how people with Asperger's experience anxiety. So far, I have listed various characteristics that would lead to increased anxiety for people with Asperger's. Once you begin to delve more deeply into the study of people with Asperger's, it becomes apparent that even among the Asperger's population, the causes of anxiety are not uniform and can, in fact, arise for entirely different reasons.

George Lynn (2007) in his book *The Asperger's Plus Child,* has listed seven different coexisting conditions (or co-morbidities) that sometimes appear alongside an Asperger's diagnosis. In addition to the seven Lynn lists, there are a few others I would like to mention. I will review the coexisting conditions that seem to be most prevalent among our population. In doing so, I will relate how each of these coexisting conditions can potentially cause anxiety for an individual.

Nonverbal Learning Disabilities

I was diagnosed with a nonverbal learning disability in addition to being diagnosed with Asperger syndrome. As Lynn points out, this unofficial diagnosis (not yet recognized by the *Diagnostic and Statistical Manual of Mental Disorders,* 4th Edition) was first researched by Byron Rourke (1989) in the 1980s. Those with a nonverbal learning disability (NLD) have what Rourke deemed right hemispheric brain dysfunction, which is to say damage to the right side of the brain. The right side of the brain is responsible for visual spatial processing, which is, in turn, responsible for interpreting the nonverbal behavior of others. The right brain is also responsible for stringing together bits and pieces of sensory data coming in from the five senses and synthesizing those details into a main idea. The Greek philosopher Aristotle would refer to this ability as "the common sense" (Hergenhahn 2005). In this case, the common sense refers to the ability to synthesize the sensory input from your five senses and simultaneously interpret the data from those senses. In other words, people with NLD have trouble taking in everything at once and might appear to lack common sense.

The left brain, responsible for details, excels for those with NLD and tends to overcompensate (Lynn 2007) for the deficits of the right brain. In doing so, the person with NLD becomes very proficient with rote learning and memorization but tends to struggle with mathematics and science. People with NLD (unlike many individuals with Asperger's and high functioning autism) tend to be auditory learners.

Already, I'm sure you can understand why it is important to delineate between these differences. We know a lot of individuals with Asperger's tend to be scientifically and mathematically oriented, but this isn't usually true for the NLD person. Yet the person with NLD will often have a coexisting diagnosis of Asperger's. Those with NLD are usually auditory learners, while we tend to think of those with Asperger's as generally being visual learners. Therefore, people with NLD and Asperger's have a unique set of challenges and abilities.

Let's look at one of the challenges that can lead to daily anxiety. If you have NLD (determined by a neuropsychological assessment), you probably have difficultly in labeling your own emotions, a condition called alexithymia. According to Lynn (2007), people with nonverbal learning disabilities have extremely rich emotional lives, but often have trouble finding the right words to describe their feelings. This is due to a cross-circuitry problem between the right and left hemispheres of the brain. The right brain isn't properly able to communicate to the left brain what you are feeling, so the left brain is saying to the right brain, "What is it that you're trying to communicate to me? What is the emotion you are experiencing? You're not making it easy for me to put words to the emotion you are experiencing."

Poor emotional recognition is anxiety provoking because feelings become difficult to interpret, subject to confusion and ambiguity. The confusion and ambiguity, in turn, create anxiety.

I suffer from this deficiency. My emotions run deep, but I often have a hard time recognizing what I'm feeling. Ultimately, I become conscious that the source of my anxiety is in not knowing what I'm feeling, which makes me even more anxious.

Emotions are complex and sometimes you may experience several different emotions simultaneously. If that wasn't enough to handle, you can also experience conflicting emotions simultaneously. You may feel jealous of your best friend, yet you simultaneously love this person as a friend. Perhaps the jealously becomes so strong that your love for this person seems obscured, yet in reality, the love is still heartfelt. Without someone pointing out these conflicting feelings out to you, it's possible that you may actually trick yourself into believing that you no longer love this person as a friend when, in fact, you do. If you have poor emotional awareness, it is challenging to understand multiple and conflicting emotions.

In my opinion, seeking professional help from a humanistic psycho-therapist in the tradition of Carl Rogers (Rogers 1961) would be benefi-cial toward improving your emotional awareness. It's a starting point for learning to recognize your feelings. A good humanistic psychotherapist is extremely skilled at interpreting your emotional states. These therapists not only listen intently to every word you have to say, but they also care-fully observe your overall nonverbal communication and then reflect back to you their interpretation of how you might be feeling. They help you understand how you feel even if you lack that clarity. They are also effec-tive in helping you sift and sort through multiple and conflicting emo-tions. One thing to know about humanistic psychologists is they pride themselves on being empathetic. These therapists will provide you with a nurturing environment in which you are unconditionally accepted for who you are. There is never any need to censor your feelings for fear of being judged. You may not always get that same kind of unconditional positive respect and empathy from a cognitive-behavioral therapist (CBT) or a psychoanalyst, though I will talk about the benefits of CBT for the Asperger's population later on.

Typically, humanistic psychotherapists will make these types of statements:

"Jake, it sounds to me what your father did several weeks ago has caused you a great deal of anger and resentment, but I am also observ-ing conflicting feelings because a part of you seems to be happy he did that. Is that correct?"

"Judy, what I hear you saying is you feel extremely betrayed, almost wounded by your best friend, like a dagger has pierced your heart. Is that true?"

Assuming I was the client and had poor emotional self-recognition, these statements would be very powerful because they would help me clarify my emotions. Whereas previously I worried about not being in touch with my feelings, this particular worry would likely diminish with some reflective statements on the part of the therapist that resonated with me upon reflection.

If you were to see a humanistic psychotherapist, I would suggest dis-closing your Asperger's and/or NLD and explain that recognizing your emotions does not come naturally to you. Your goal in therapy would be to become more proficient at recognizing your emotions. Therefore, you should make it clear to the therapist that you want her not only to reflect back to you how she thinks you might be feeling, but you also want her to teach you effective strategies so that you can accomplish this goal on your own.

Attention deficit disorder

A whole book could be written on how attention deficit disorder (ADD) contributes to one's high anxiety levels. Tony Attwood (2006) states that a diagnosis of AS and ADD (or ADHD) is not mutually exclusive. This is reinforced by Dr. Ghaziuddin (2005) who says that having a developmental disability (or difference) such as Asperger's naturally increases the risk of a comorbid ADD diagnosis. We spoke earlier about the characteristic of "monotropism" which is a single channeled attention span. With ADD, it is arguable that these individuals have a disregulated attention span. If you have ADD and Asperger's, chances are you find it difficult to filter out stimuli from the external world. Everything catches your attention and you may find your mind wandering, unable to focus on something for any substantial period of time. For the pure Aspie, only certain things of interest grab your attention but this is not true for the pure ADDer. For the ADDer, the mind keeps racing from one thing to the next. In practical terms, having ADD means that the person will have frequent bouts of poor concentration and focus. Keep in mind this important point: Just as it is true that an NLD individual is usually not a visual learner but still can have Asperger's, so too can someone have a different perceptual style (like ADD) and also have Asperger's. The Asperger population is not homogenous at all! Therefore, one can be diagnosed with both ADD and Asperger's simultaneously.

Having ADD is quite anxiety provoking because many people have a hard time concentrating and focusing for extended periods of time, especially on things that are of no interest to them. Problems with inattention, executive functioning and concentration effect almost all aspects of life, from work to romance to social relationships. In addition, these same problems can be frustrating when these individuals are trying to listen and be attentive to other people, remember people's names and other simple and complex cognitive tasks of daily living that require focus and attention. For someone with Asperger's who already has difficulty social-izing, if they also have ADD, the problem is now compounded by certain cognitive and perceptual issues that can compromise one's ability to suc-ceed in a number of different venues.

Because I am not a medical doctor, I will not delve into the medica-tions that are useful for the ADD population. Obviously, there has been a lot of informative material written on this issue by many reputable doc-tors and psychologists. All I can say is that if you feel that taking a medi-cation to help with your focus and concentration might be helpful, you should be open to the idea. With that said, it would be useful to find a psychiatrist or medical doctor, who has areas of specialization in both the autism spectrum and ADD.

Obsessive-compulsive disorder

Obsessive-compulsive disorder (OCD) is another condition that often exists alongside Asperger's. Attwood (2006) estimates that 25 per cent of those diagnosed with Asperger's also have OCD. Lynn (2007) lists this as one of his seven coexisting conditions.

In Chapter 1, I spoke of alien hand syndrome and panic attacks as automatic physiological reactions that are beyond a person's conscious control. In the case of OCD, this happens in the form of intrusive thoughts. The thoughts act as the metaphoric alien hand because they are intrusive and automatic by nature. In other words, they seemingly occur with or without your conscious permission. A person with OCD has these intru-sive thoughts so often that it begins to affect one's behavior by taking on the form of compulsions. According to Attwood (2006), the intrusive thoughts of most people with Asperger's center around the preoccupation of making a mistake.

Someone with Asperger's and OCD is even more monotropic and hyper-vigilant than the person with just Asperger's. It's easy to see how having both OCD and Asperger's would create significant anxiety in one's life. You may constantly worry that if you don't do a particular act ritualistically, something terrible might happen. For that extra bit of reas-surance, you may check ten or more times to make sure you locked the door before you leave your house. Perhaps you have become hypersensi-tive to criticism or obsessed with having to do a perfect job or your worst fear will come true.

The most debilitating aspect of OCD is the intrusiveness of the thoughts. If the outside world wasn't confusing enough, now you have an inner world that's just as confusing, if not more so. It's hard to relax when confronted by both OCD and Asperger's. According to Attwood (2006), treatment for OCD usually involves a combination of medication and CBT, which we will discuss in its own chapter.

Schizoid personality disorder

This is not one of Lynn's seven coexisting conditions, and yet I feel it is important to mention because research has shown it can occur alongside Asperger's (Wolff 1995), though it is relatively unusual. There is enough overlap between schizoids and "Aspies", though, to warrant some discussion on the subject.

For someone with schizoid personality disorder, he or she feels most content being alone. Social interactions for this person are very taxing and create a sense of feeling engulfed. Daily life situations that involve relationships, such as work and marriage are incredibly grueling. You can think of this type of person as an extreme introvert. While most introverts do not mind socializing once in a while, the schizoid sees socializing as an unnecessary burden to be avoided at all costs.

Even though I don't consider myself to have schizoid personality disorder, I can be somewhat of a loner. In the March 2008 edition of the *Autism-Asperger's Digest,* I wrote an article about spending time alone and not being ashamed of it. In that article, I made clear that many people with Asperger syndrome are not loners. In fact, a significant number of people with Asperger's desperately want social interactions but may find the nuances of socializing difficult. True loners—or schizoids—on the other hand, are content being by themselves. For a book that helps the loner accept him- or herself, please refer to Anneli Rufus' *Party of One: The Loner's Manifesto* (Rufus 2003).

It is easy to see how the loners among the Asperger's population experience anxiety. We live in a culture that glorifies being with other people and attempts to paint solitude as a sad endeavor. The pressure our families and society put on us to socialize, when really we prefer our own company, is enormous. For those individuals inclined to be by themselves, they learn from an early age this is wrong, unhealthy, and unproductive. Think about it. Most parents want their children to get married or be in a relationship. Most schools house children more than half the year for six hours a day, a real nightmare for any schizoid. Then after school, there are more activities involving socializing. As adults, we shuffle off to our 9 to 5 jobs where we interact with people all day. Many of us then come home to families who expect us to meet other social needs. The actual amount of time most people spend by themselves is minimal, even for those with schizoid personality disorders.

If you are a schizoid, I offer a word of advice: accept your solitary lifestyle and avoid societal pressures to conform or pressures that don't fit with your authentic self, i.e. what you believe are your real needs. I would also encourage you to find employment that is fulfilling but at the same time doesn't require constant social contact. If you're lucky, this will mean being a freelancer in some capacity of work. Or if you have to work with people, be sure to give yourself plenty of down time between going to work and coming home so you can restore your form and recharge your battery.

Depression

Observing the children who displayed the characteristics of his syndrome, Hans Asperger (1994) noted they also displayed features of depression (Ghaziuddin 2005). There are various grades or levels of depression, and some are more serious than others. Dysthymia is a low-grade depression, meaning it's less intense than major depression. For a person to have dysthymia, he or she must experience symptoms related to depression for at least two years. If you have dysthymia, chances are you are already aware that something is not right with your mood. Perhaps you experience symptoms including irritability, overeating, or problems falling asleep.

In talking to others with Asperger's, my anecdotal experience suggests many of us experience dysthymia. This makes sense to me. I believe anxiety and depression reinforce each other. When you are anxious, you tend to become depressed that life isn't easier than it is, but when you're depressed, you become anxious things will never change and you'll always remain melancholy. This is why it is not uncommon for a person to have both an anxiety disorder and a mood disorder like depression or low-grade depression such as dysthymia. The two often go hand in hand.

Let me conclude this chapter by reinforcing a point I made at the outset of Chapter 2. Yes, life for a person with Asperger's tends to include more than its fair share of anxiety for the reasons already mentioned, and it is quite easy to take pity on one's self or feel more anxious. But that's not what this book is advocating. The rest of this book will arm you with clear strategies to help you reduce anxiety in all facets of your life.

Action points

- Instead of viewing the world as a dangerous place, view yourself as a brave warrior heading into battle. Reframe the situation from negative to positive.

- Be aware that certain environmental triggers (such as being hypersensitive) can make you more anxious. Place yourself in environments that are most conducive to your needs.

- Anxiety and monotropism are related, so try not to become too narrowly focused on individual pieces of information.

- Try not to be perfectionistic to the point where you feel anxious if you don't do something perfectly.

Chapter 3

Cognitive-behavioral therapy

One morning I went to the bookstore to look for some stimulating reading material. As I was leaving the bookstore, I accidentally backed into another car in the parking lot and caused some minor damage to it. After exchanging obligatory information with the other driver, I had a choice as to how I could conceptualize this incident in my mind. On the one hand, I could tell myself:

"You careless fool!"

"This so typical of you, Nick. You always screw things up."

"The other driver must think you're a total idiot."

Or, I could reframe the situation and tell myself the following:

"This happens to many people at one point in time. Besides, this isn't something you do very often, Nick. When was the last time you were in a car accident? Never."

"Give yourself a break. No one is perfect."

"Let's look at the bright side. No one got hurt, and the damage was minor."

These interior monologues describe the same situation, but they employ two very different perceptions of the same event. In essence, that's the whole point of cognitive-behavioral therapy (CBT). By using CBT techniques, you can begin to look at situations in an entirely different way, thereby reducing high anxiety. That's what this chapter is about.

A couple of caveats before we begin: this chapter contains some weighty material certain readers might find overwhelming. There is a lot of information in this chapter, and for someone new to cognitive-behavioral therapy, some of this material may be challenging and difficult to read. There are two reasons why I chose to present the content for this chapter. The first reason is that you won't find this material in other self-help books geared toward adults with Asperger syndrome. I strongly believe it's time our population had access to this information in a book solely devoted to Asperger's. The second reason is this information goes beyond lip service to offer you concrete ways to take control of your anxiety. If you have had trouble controlling your anxiety, realize that it is not your fault.

For a long time, I blamed myself for being as anxious as I was. I simply never learned how to control my anxiety, and I didn't factor into the equation my Asperger's, a neurological difference that made my challenges much different from others. The same is probably true for you. You may have never learned exactly how to control your anxiety, either on your own or with someone's help. After all, emotional awareness and anxiety control isn't generally a part of a curriculum in most schools.

Mastering emotions and controlling anxiety are skills. Very few people are born knowing how to control anxiety (unless you are born with an extremely calm temperament). Like any skill, you can't just be expected to know it instinctively. For example, it is unlikely you could learn the skills of karate by trial and error. Rather, you would probably require instruction from a teacher skilled in the martial arts. You would need guidance to master the techniques involved. There are also techniques involved for mastering your thoughts or emotions and controlling your anxiety. And of course, practicing these techniques is essential. Admittedly, learning and implementing these techniques will take hard work and dedication, but I promise you it is learnable.

In this chapter and in this book, we go beyond platitudes. I won't just tell you to change your thoughts. I provide strategies and examples of *how* you can change your thoughts to master your emotions and lower anxiety levels. The majority of this chapter focuses on CBT. The end of the chapter and subsequent chapters will put this information in a useful "Aspergerian" context, in which you can begin to apply this information to your everyday life.

Cognitive-behavioral therapy has been especially effective in helping people manage their anxiety. Specifically, it has been shown to be helpful with the Asperger's population (Gaus 2007). In this chapter, I am going to cover some self-help tips for applying CBT. I'd like to discuss why I believe using CBT can be an especially effective tool in your own life. Let me give you a few brief examples I hope will illustrate the potential transformational power of CBT.

Try on a new pair of glasses

I used to have 20/20 vision. In fact, better than 20/20 vision. As a child, I would routinely boast about clearly reading highway road signs at great distances when my parents could barely see the signs. My excellent eyesight contributed to my becoming an effective tennis player. I wasn't even aware of the changes that were taking place when my vision was in a state of gradual decline. Was I oblivious to something as obvious as my own eyesight changing? The fact is, I had slowly grown accustomed to the gradual changes in my vision so after awhile, I came to accept my declining vision as being the norm, even though it was not as good as when my vision was 20/20. From my view, my eyesight had not changed, even though I couldn't read those road signs anymore.

Here is how I came to realize my distance vision was declining. I went in for a routine eye exam. It was my first eye exam in eight or nine years. Upon noticing that I had missed some letters in the eye chart, the optometrist informed me that I was nearsighted. I couldn't (or didn't want to) believe him. My vision seemed fine to me. Better than fine, actually. I was still driving, playing tennis, and engaging in other normal activities. I assumed this doctor didn't know what he was talking about. Nevertheless, he did the unthinkable, as far as I was concerned: he gave me a prescription for a pair of glasses. I was shocked. At the age of 30, for the first time in my life, a doctor told me I needed glasses. "Well, okay,

I'll humor the guy. I'll try on a pair and politely tell him they didn't make any difference," I thought to myself. Do you know what happened? I put on the glasses and my distance vision became ten times better. Wait a minute? That meant my distance vision wasn't as good as I thought it was after all. How could I not have known?

Now, it's amazing to me how blurry things look without the glasses. I won't go anywhere without them. The reality of my perception about my eyesight has changed.

I equate how I was experiencing problems with distance vision (and not realizing it) with a person who regularly misjudges situations but lacks the ability to realize it. Just because you have Asperger's doesn't mean you can't learn the skills to discern reality with a clearer lens. When you put on your metaphoric new pair of glasses, as I'm inviting you to do, you'll be pleasantly surprised at how much clearer and simpler your view of your life will become. This clarity will also mean life will become a lot less anxiety-filled for you. When you engage in this process, you will gain more peace, serenity, and greater mastery over your emotions.

You may think it is presumptuous of me to tell you some of your perceptions may actually be wrong and may be the source of much of your anxiety. Let me assure you that all people, from time to time, misjudge reality. We, as human beings, tend to magnify a situation or we may entirely misread a situation, such as a social cue. However, I do believe that despite the high intelligence among individuals with Asperger's, because of our black-and-white thinking and monotropism, we are more likely to misjudge reality. This is not in any way intended as an insult. After all, we "spectrumites," as Michael John Carley, executive director of GRASP, The Global and Regional Asperger Syndrome Partnership, would say, have certain special abilities that neurotypicals would love to have.

Blind spots

Cognitive-behavioral therapists are not the only ones to recognize that people have a tendency to misinterpret their external reality. Even the ancient Greeks were aware of this. The philosopher Plato (2004) in his *Allegory of the Cave* from *The Republic* recognized that people can sometimes be tricked into believing things that simply aren't true. Imagine the only reality you have ever known is that you are tied to a chair, facing the wall of a cave. Your head and limbs are chained so you cannot move. Behind you, there is a huge fire. Between the fire and where you are sitting is a raised walkway where various puppets are being projected onto the wall of the cave, creating shadows on the wall you face. If you were never able to turn your head and recognize what was causing the shadows on the wall, you might very well come to accept the shadows as coming from real people or animals. After all, if you were never exposed to any other reality, wouldn't it seem rational to think the shadows were more than puppets?

A more realistic example is that of the blind spot when you are driving. You think you can clearly see the road around you. That is your sense of your external reality, but there are small areas that are blocked from your view—areas of the road that cannot be seen while looking forward or with the side or rearview mirrors. Blind spots can also occur in real life, where we can't see something that's right under our nose. CBT helps you to uncover those blind spots.

Take a look at the passage below and try to count the number of f's. Look at this sentence just once, and don't read beyond it:

FINISHED FILES ARE THE RE-
SULT OF YEARS OF SCIENTIF-
IC STUDY COMBINED WITH
THE EXPERIENCE OF YEARS.

This passage has circulated on the Internet but no one claims ownership of it. If you are like most people, you probably counted three f's from the above sentence. I have demonstrated this exercise with several audiences when I present at conferences and most everyone in the audience counts three f's. When I first saw it and subsequently learned there are actually six f's, I didn't believe it at first. Maybe you don't believe it either. Let's look at it again:

> FINISHED FILES ARE THE RE-
> SULT OF YEARS OF SCIENTIF-
> IC STUDY COMBINED WITH
> THE EXPERIENCE OF YEARS.

Amazing, isn't it? What happens is the brain usually interprets the *f* in "of" as a *v* and completely bypasses an awareness of the *f*. So while there are indeed six f's in the sentence, the brain usually only sees three. Some of you may have counted six f's, and if you did, it means you have an extraordinary ability to hone in on details. However, I am sure that most of you only counted three f's.

My point is to suggest how easy it is for people to misconstrue their external reality. If our brains skip over something as obvious as seeing an *f*, think about what else we might also misconstrue.

Often, your thoughts and feelings will be based on certain percep- tions that simply aren't accurate because of blind spots or because of long- held, false assumptions. You may be like one of Plato's prisoners. Having believed something to be true for so long, it's almost impossible for you to believe anything to the contrary because it's the only reality you've ever known. You may be like the driver who simply can't see the car in the next lane because of a blind spot. Ultimately, you may base your actions on distorted and maladaptive cognitions (thoughts) that are inac- curate and work against your best interests. CBT helps remove ingrained, maladaptive thought patterns and the more benign blind spots that often accompany them.

The precepts of CBT

CBT or self-therapy forces you to take a look at your thoughts the way a scientist would examine something under a microscope. It assumes once you change your cognitions to match that of your external reality more appropriately, your behavior will change to correspond to the new, reality- based thoughts. In CBT your thoughts directly influence your behavior.

One of the most basic precepts of CBT is you should behave like a scientist when examining your thoughts (Branch and Wilson 2006). Behaving like a scientist sounds like it would be well suited to the apti- tude of someone with Asperger's, right? Yes and no. Although it is true many people with Asperger's possess an inquiring mind that can lead to appropriate scientific inquiry, they usually have a harder time using this skill when it comes to their own thoughts and feelings. Yet, that is exactly what I'm going to challenge you to do in this chapter and throughout the rest of the book.

The second basic precept of CBT is habitual or long-held thoughts will greatly influence your feelings and, ultimately, your behavior. The longer you carry around thoughts that inaccurately reflect your external reality, the more sway or influence those thoughts will have over your emotional state. For example, if I continue to think that I'm an idiot and a terrible writer, I'll begin to experience feelings of doubt, shame and low self-esteem if I want to write something. Conversely, if I think I am the best author in the world (which I'm not), I'll begin to feel grandiose about myself and angry with others who write negative reviews of my books on amazon.com. The aim of CBT is to consciously monitor your thoughts and then decide if those thoughts accurately match up with the reality of the situation.

Getting back to "behaving like a scientist," what do I mean? If you were conducting a scientific experiment, you would want to be as objective as possible with your data. A big challenge many beginning scientists experience when performing an experiment is not letting their own biases guide their research. The scientist must prevent her emotions from dictating the findings of her research. As a CBT self-therapist/scientist, your challenge will be to look at your thoughts with the same objectivity as a scientist would when collecting data or interpreting the results of the data. Will this be easy? Heck no! It particularly won't be easy for the Asperger's population reading this book, who tends to have trouble with seeing the whole picture. But in order to view our thoughts with as much objectivity as possible, it's going to be essential for us to step back and try to view as much of the big picture as possible.

Magnification

Suppose you go into a meeting with a work supervisor and feel vulnerable about your performance of late. At the meeting, the boss criticizes you regarding a number of areas in which you need to improve. It would be easy for you to come out of that meeting thinking things like:

"I'm a failure."

"The boss hates me."

"I'll be lucky if I don't get fired within the next two weeks."

What kind of feelings would soon follow those three thoughts? Disgust, shame, depression and most certainly, anxiety. You might become scared about losing your job to the point where you exhibit paranoia any time you see your boss. If you stepped back and viewed this situation more objectively, like a scientist would, you might say to yourself:

"This is highly unusual for my boss to give me criticism. In fact, in five years, this is only the third time it has happened."

"My boss values my work ethic because he's complimented me many times in the past."

"Sure, I was lambasted today, but a lot of other good employees who work at this company have also been treated in this manner at various times."

Do you see the difference between the first three statements and the last three? The first three statements were *not* based on facts. Rather, they were based on illogical assumptions. The second set of statements are based solely on facts that then provide some breathing room to step back and examine the big picture with more objectivity. Should you choose to focus only on what happened today (the boss criticized you), it's easy to form false assumptions and convince yourself that you may, indeed, be fired. However, should you choose to step back, look at the totality of the situation, and analyze the past actions of your boss, it's easy to see how the fear dismissal is not reality-based. All the energy you spent worrying about being fired is unnecessary. Analyzing what happened today with your boss without taking into account past actions of his behavior is an example of what David Burns (1980) calls *magnification*. You are magnifying the situation entirely out of proportion instead of viewing the situation in the totality of the circumstances. When you magnify any object, by definition you are then able to concentrate on the small details rather than focus on the larger object. Magnifying a particular life situation, which creates the same consequences as magnifying an object, is something that people with Asperger's have a propensity to do.

Cognitive distortions

Magnification is only one of ten cognitive distortions identified by Burns (1980) in his groundbreaking book, *Feeling Good*. Even though Burns identified these ten distortions as the basis for nearly all depressive symptoms, I think the same could be said of anxiety when referring to these distortions. *A* cognitive distortion is an illogical assumption you make about a particular situation.

Truthfully, everyone employs the use of these distortions on a semi-regular basis so please do not get the impression that I am singling out the Asperger's population here. However, I do believe that your overall problems with central coherence will make it more likely that you'll be more prone to using these distortions more often, despite your otherwise high intellect. What these distortions have in common is they all force you to fall into the trap of rigid and narrow thinking. They convince you certain thoughts are true, based on a limited amount of available evidence. As a result of being monotropic and probably focusing on the small details of any given situation, these distortions make it even more enticing to focus on the smaller details. It becomes another never-ending cycle if you let it.

Each of these cognitive distortions represents a natural human impulse. Even the most intelligent human beings will use these distortions from time to time. They appear to be universal. To become acquainted with these distortions is the first step toward becoming consciously aware you are using them. Once you know you are employing a particular distortion, you can reframe the situation in your mind so it matches up with the reality of the situation.

Reframing means to look at a situation in a new light, or in a more accurate light. In the example of my car accident, I could have erroneously chosen to believe I was an idiot because I hit a car and magnified the situation. Or I could have reframed the situation by examining it objectively.

I could have considered the fact I rarely get into car accidents and am normally a good driver, so I'm really not an idiot after all.

Let's go through some (not all) of these cognitive distortions Burns (1980) presents and examine their meaning. Each of these examples is my own. The definitions are paraphrased from Burns.

Cognitive distortion #1: All or nothing thinking

Definition: all or nothing thinking causes a person to evaluate certain characteristics in terms of whether something is all "good" or all "bad".

> Jenny is an expert chef who happens to overcook a chicken dinner one night. Based on this one dinner, Jenny concludes that she is a terrible chef. Instead of recognizing her past accomplishments, Jenny chooses to focus on this one mistake (magnification) and concludes she is a lousy chef. She believes she can either be a "perfect" chef or a "lousy" chef. That there is no middle ground.

- How might this cognitive distortion (internal problem) provoke future anxiety for Jenny? Jenny's identity stems from the fact she is a fantastic chef. Now that she has cooked a bad meal, she secretly questions whether she really deserves to be called an expert chef.

- What's the problem? Jenny has suffered a blow to her self-esteem and may decide to give up cooking.

- What's the distortion from Jenny's point of view? "One bad meal equals one bad chef."

Cognitive reframing: Jenny is not a perfect chef (an impossible standard to meet), but she is a very good one.

Cognitive distortion #2: Overgeneralization

Definition: to overgeneralize is to take one situation that occurred and to conclude falsely the same situation is bound to happen over and over.

- Jenny concludes her one bad meal is likely to lead to other bad meals in the future.

- How might this cognitive distortion provoke future anxiety for Jenny? She may become very nervous about the quality of her cooking in the future.

- What's the problem? Same as #1.

- What's the distortion from Jenny's point of view? "Because I cooked a bad meal, I'm going to cook more bad meals in the future."

Cognitive reframing: Jenny has rarely, if ever, cooked a bad meal. In reality, it is not likely to occur again.

Cognitive distortion #3: Disqualifying the positive

Definition: to disqualify the positive is to ignore the positive aspects of a situation and only choose to focus on the negative ones.

> Nick Dubin has just finished giving a presentation to a group of 180 people. Afterward, Nick looks at his evaluation forms. One hundred and seventy-six of them are positive. Four evaluation forms, however, offer some critical comments. Nick concludes that he gave a terrible presentation on the basis of the four critical responses. (This is a true example.)

- How might this cognitive distortion provoke future anxiety for Nick? Nick may become hypersensitive to criticism.

- What's the problem? Nick may decide to give up public speaking.

- What's the distortion from Nick's point of view? "If anyone criticizes my performance, it must either mean I'm a poor speaker or my presentation was not as effective as I hoped it would be."

Cognitive reframing: It is an impossible task to try and please everybody all the time. Just because a handful of people think Nick gave an imperfect presentation doesn't mean he did. Maybe the criticism can even be helpful in future presentations.

Cognitive distortion #4: "Fortune telling"

Definition: to fall into the trap of "fortune telling" is to assume that you have the ability to predict the future.

> Daryl, a man with Asperger's, has been on several dates in which the woman did not want a second date. This weekend, Daryl has a date with another young woman. However, Daryl erroneously predicts this next date will be a flop because the preceding ones did not go well.

- How might this cognitive distortion provoke anxiety for Daryl? He will become extremely nervous about his date this weekend.

- What is the problem? Daryl might stop dating.

- What's the distortion from Daryl's point of view? "Anyone who has been rejected several times in a row will never get a girlfriend. Therefore, since I have been rejected multiple times, this next date is hopeless."

Cognitive reframing: Many people suffer repeated rejections before meeting the right person. Daryl's situation isn't unusual at all, but because it's emotionally painful to him, it feels unusual to him. Furthermore, let's assume Daryl now uses his Asperger's as a way to predict he will never get married. This would be an erroneous prediction as well, since many individuals with Asperger's ultimately find a spouse or domestic partner.

Cognitive distortion #5: The should/must trap

Definition: A person who falls into this trap has unrealistic expectations of herself and others. The psychologist Albert Ellis (Burns 1980) called this distortion "musturbation," in that a person thinks things "should" or "must" be a certain way. "That person should nice to me." "I must be an all-A student." A cognitive-behavioral therapist would ask you to think about what would happen if someone wasn't nice to you. Would that really be the worst thing to happen to you? If you didn't receive all A's, would that be so terrible? Falling into this trap will almost guarantee you seek perfectionism in yourself and others, leading to a constant state of anxiety.

- Jenny thinks she should never make a bad meal.

- Nick thinks everyone who ever attends his presentations should enjoy them thoroughly.

- Daryl believes he should never suffer a personal rejection when dating.

How might these cognitive distortions provoke anxiety for Jenny, Nick, and Daryl? Jenny will have impossible perfectionist standards when it comes to her cooking and will be worried about not living up to those standards. Nick will worry profusely about other people's opinions when it comes to his presentations. Daryl will worry about being rejected and will try too hard to make his dates like him.

What are the distortions from Jenny, Nick, and Daryl's point of view? Jenny believes, "A good chef should never cook a bad meal." Daryl thinks, "A likeable date should never be rejected."

Nick feels, "A good presenter should never be criticized by anyone."

Cognitive reframing: For Jenny, good chefs are bound to have their off-days. It is impossible to expect perfect results every single time. Daryl needs to realize a string of rejections does not mean he is destined to be alone. Nick comes to understand everyone receives criticism. As a public speaker, he must be able to endure some criticism.

Cognitive distortion #6: Personalization

Definition: To personalize something is to blame yourself for a seemingly random event.

> Professor Wilkinson teaches anthropology at a university. He has received good (though not perfect) student evaluations over the past few years. On this particular day, however, half the class didn't turn in homework assignments. Wilkinson automatically thinks this has to do with his inability to teach even though he has received positive feedback (disqualifying the positive) in the past.

- How might this cognitive distortion provoke anxiety for Wilkinson? He worries he's not getting through to his students. Perhaps he'll build up some existential anxiety by worrying he's wasting away his purpose in life since he is such a lousy professor.

- What's the problem? Wilkinson might retire early or find a different line of work not as compatible with his talents for teaching.

- What's the distortion from Wilkinson's point of view? "I am a lousy professor because my students are so unmotivated."

Cognitive reframing: Wilkinson shouldn't ascribe poor teaching as the cause of his students' behavior. After all, his students normally turn in their work, and he does get positive evaluations from his students. Perhaps there was a campus event the night before or that football game everyone was so excited about.

I hope you were able to recognize what happened in these examples when they allowed their cognitive distortions to get the better of them. Each of them retreated. Each stopped taking risks. They stopped cooking, speaking, dating, and teaching. That is what happens in real life when people have trouble dealing with their anxiety effectively. Instead of facing their anxiety head-on, people who display maladaptive coping patterns tend to run away from future perceived risks. Do you see these patterns happening in your own life? If so, it's okay. Once you recognize patterns, they can be changed.

It's unrealistic to suggest you will never fall into the trap of using some of these distortions. I guarantee you will. We all will, but now that you know what these distortions are, you have the ability to recognize when you are using them and consciously shift your thinking when it happens. You now have the ability to reframe your thoughts to confront your anxiety. Being unaware you are using these distortions is like walking through life wearing a blindfold. As long as you have the blindfold on, you don't have to face your fear.

I encourage you to review the list of cognitive distortions before moving on to the next section.

Emotions and thoughts are intertwined

Your thoughts will often reflect your current emotional state. If you are feeling sad or depressed during a given period, it's likely many of your thoughts will relate to your sadness. As long as you are feeling sad, you'll be thinking sad thoughts, whether you want to or not. This sounds pessimistic, and it is, only if you think your thoughts have the power to control you, rather than *you* being in control of your thoughts. As long as you are unaware of your thought patterns during times of emotional distress, they will continue to control you. Once you become aware of these thoughts, not only can you learn to recognize cognitive distortions, but you can also begin to master them by consciously rejecting them. This approach begs an important question: if you change your thoughts, does that mean you learn to change your emotional state at will? The short answer is yes. More on this shortly.

Cognitive distortions often operate unconsciously because many thoughts are unconscious. Nonetheless, they do influence you. Think of subliminal advertising: if a product is momentarily visible in a movie (an actor drinking from a bottle of Coca-Cola), it can influence individuals to buy that product. Similarly, your own thoughts (which you have access to 24 hours a day) influence your behavior through subliminal messages. In fact, your mind is the ultimate subliminal machine.

Think about how the limbic system and particularly the amygdala can hijack your behavior under certain circumstances (we referred to this earlier as "emotional hijacking"). That's exactly how the subliminal messaging system works in your mind. The emotional brain is so quick to respond, it overrides your higher-order thinking to employ the use of these cognitive distortions before you've even had a chance to figure out what's happened. The goal of CBT is to get you to slow down once the stressor has passed so you can contemplate these situations via the thinking part of the brain versus the emotional part of the brain. I'm not saying you should try to suppress your emotions but the rational part of your brain is there for a reason!

Think of the neocortex as the "scientist" and your amygdala as the "first alert system" of your mind. The first alert system is useful and necessary to alert you to real danger, but thereafter, you do not want it to create false alarms based on imagined dangers. What good would a smoke detector be if it went off constantly for no good reason? The more susceptible you are to the subliminal messages of your mind, the more false alarms you will have. The more false alarms you experience, the more anxiety you are likely to have on a daily basis.

You are also likely to be more monotropic the more you are swayed by your subliminal messaging system. This makes sense. Each one of these cognitive distortions forces you to fall into the trap of narrow-minded thinking, which is what monotropism is. If you are narrow-minded, without any awareness of the subliminal messages, doesn't it make sense your monotropism will become more dominant? If there were a technique that helped you become more aware of the subliminal messages, wouldn't you want to take advantage of it? CBT is a technique that helps you "tune in" to those subliminal messages.

If these cognitive distortions have been a pattern of your unconscious, you may have arrived at a point where acting on them has become second nature to you. In other words, you use these distortions without even thinking about it. The point of cognitive-behavioral therapy is to get you to slow down and take note of your emotions and thoughts so you can consciously be aware of the distortions in your thought patterns.

Can we control our emotions?

Do emotions exist as an inevitable state of our being or can we control them voluntarily? If certain emotions and thoughts are subliminal, can we respond to them with any real conscious intent? This question has been debated among researchers who study human emotions. Some researchers who, from a purely biological point of view, think emotions are determined mainly by our subcortical (limbic) activity, which largely escapes conscious control (Reeve 2004). However, another set of theorists believe human beings have conscious control over their feelings and emotions. These theorists study emotions from a cognitive point of view and are called appraisal theorists.

Cognitive appraisal

I'm now going to detail how your subliminal message system works. By understanding how the process of cognitive appraisal works, you will learn some secrets about the inner workings on your mind.

A basic tenet of appraisal theory is that emotions do not occur without something from the outside (external) world triggering them (Reeve 2004). If someone commanded you to "feel joy", you would ask, "About what?" But there's a twist to this inquiry. In appraisal theory, the thing that triggers an emotion is not the cause of the emotion itself but your appraisal of that thing is. Think of the word "appraisal" as being like "assessment".

An example Reeve (2004) gives is that of a child who sees a stranger approaching. It isn't the man approaching the child that causes the child to become anxious. It's the meaning the child attaches to the man that causes him to become anxious. As Reeve says, the child assesses the facial expressions of the man, what he's been taught about strangers, gender, pace of the approach, etc. The child then appraises whether this situation is good or bad and acts accordingly. If he views it as good, the child would obviously act much differently than if he views it as bad.

Richard Lazarus (1991) takes the concept of appraisal a step further. In Lazarus's view, people ask themselves a set of questions related to their appraisal of a situation. In addition to asking whether the situation is good or bad, we typically assess whether the stressor being imposed on us actually relates to our well-being. As with the case of the child, his well-being may be threatened if the stranger has ill intentions, and the child knows this threat exists. If the man was merely walking down the street, the child would not have any emotion because the man would pose no threat to his well-being. In some ways, the outside stressor must be relevant to our own well-being.

Lazarus says we ask ourselves if the stressor impinges upon or helps us to achieve our goals. From the previous example, if the child's goal is to walk home from school and he thinks the stranger might frustrate his goal, he's going to experience anxiety. In addition to being concerned about our well-being, we ask ourselves if the stressor will damage or help enhance our self-esteem in any way.

Primary appraisal

All of these questions float around in your mind instantaneously and are usually controlled by the amygdala, again giving you very little time, if any, to react. Primary appraisal is when the brain first generates and appraises these questions (Lazarus and Folkman 1984). It's called primary appraisal because it's literally your first chance to assess the situation. During the primary appraisal process, you immediately assess such things as your physical well-being, self-esteem, a current goal, financial security, etc. If a mugger was about to rob you, your goals of getting home safely, your financial security, and even your self-esteem might be jeopardized. Of course, you are not consciously thinking about these things in the moment, but this is what is motivating you to get away from the mugger.

You want to keep your money; you want to make it home, etc. It's important to understand primary appraisal happens so fast it's virtually impossible to be aware of it as it is happening. Nonetheless, it does occur.

The primary appraisal process assesses the following:

1. Is something relevant to your well-being? If it is, you take immediate action and generate an emotion. If it is not, you go about the rest of your day.

2. If there is a threat to your well-being that seems insurmountable, you are likely to avoid the situation, like fleeing from a mugger.

3. If there is a threat to your well-being in which you determine you can face the threat, you're likely to deal with the threat directly.

Secondary appraisal

It is during the secondary appraisal phase that most cognitive distortions take place. For something to reach secondary appraisal, you must have determined in the primary appraisal phase that something is causing you stress. If you felt the stress was a result of a distortion in the first place, then secondary appraisal will not occur.

During the secondary appraisal phase, time has passed between the actual stressor and your assessment of it. With the danger having passed (the mugger or the stranger are gone), you can consciously assess the situation. Secondary appraisal involves what you tell yourself about the situation and how you cope with it. The coping mechanisms you employ are based on your assessment of the situation. If you deem a situation hopeless, you are less likely to cope effectively than if you think you can take some kind of action about it.

The difference between primary and secondary appraisal

Assume someone is mugging you. This is the primary appraisal process likely to take place:

"Oh my God, I may die!"

"He looks mean and threatening. I don't want to end up in the hospital!"

"I love my family. I may never see them again!"

Again, you're not actually thinking these things consciously, but you are thinking about them unconsciously, and this is what motivates you to run from the mugger.

Secondary appraisal of the situation would involve statements like:

"Boy, I'm an idiot for having my wallet sticking out my pocket. I'm so stupid."

"I will learn from this situation and keep my wallet in a less conspicuous place."

Let's look at the two secondary appraisal statements. The first one will lead to the emotions of shame, disgust, and further anxiety, while the second statement will lead to greater confidence in one's abilities to stay clear of danger in the future. The two pairs of statements lead to two entirely different ways of coping with the situation.

Core beliefs

Unlike primary appraisal, which is mostly unconscious, secondary appraisal should be a conscious process but often isn't. For the individual who called himself an idiot for being robbed, perhaps he's called himself an idiot so many times in the past it has become part of his self-identity. He accepts this negative self-image as the truth. During secondary appraisal, he doesn't rationally assess whether or not he's an idiot. He just accepts the fact he is one. This negative self-image has become a *core belief* for the individual, and it's a belief he's probably had since he was a child.

As Jeffery Young states, core beliefs usually form in childhood (Klosko, Weishaar and Young 2006) and are reinforced by cognitive distortions. What happened during childhood is you gradually convinced yourself something was true, so you no longer needed to question whether it was true as you progressed into adulthood. Once a core belief forms, second-ary appraisal simply goes through the motions because you are not open to other possibilities. Katie, a fellow classmate of mine, calls this a "crisis of imagination", or lack of imagination. Once something becomes a core belief, it's hard think otherwise, despite evidence to the contrary. You cannot envision any other possibilities. You merely accept the core belief as a conclusive fact, like the sky is blue or the sun sets in the west.

If you formed negative core beliefs about yourself in childhood and continue to accept those beliefs in adulthood, you're limiting the way you assess situations and closing yourself off from a more rational, adult point of view. This is exactly how the subliminal messaging system works. It tells you, "Of course this is the way it is. It can't be any other way." The core beliefs you hold about yourself or the world automatically negate any other possibilities. It is like a 12th-century farmer saying, "The world is flat. What is there to discuss? I'm certain this is the truth." It's highly unlikely he would have been open to discussing the possibility that, per-haps, the world wasn't flat. The secondary appraisal process is meaning-less. It is inconceivable there could be any other truth. In the case of the man who is being robbed, he might unconsciously think something like, "Sure, I'm an idiot for being mugged. What other explanation is there?" Lacking a flexible thought process is dangerous because it leads to nega-tive emotions. It is during secondary appraisal you actually have a chance to slow yourself down and prevent these cognitive distortions. But if you have already formed core beliefs, you have virtually no chance of catching cognitive distortions. Their purpose is to reinforce your core beliefs.

Here are examples of some negative core beliefs:

The world is an unfair place.

I am worthless.

People cannot be trusted.

These are all negative core beliefs based on certain cognitive distortions that have formed and been reinforced repeatedly. A negative core belief is a giant cognitive distortion that has been accepted as fact, without any questioning or critical thinking surrounding it. It's what I like to call "dis-tortion dogma". Secondary appraisal loses its purpose once these negative core beliefs solidify. The core beliefs serve as roadblocks barring the way for thoughtful alternatives. Once a person forms negative core beliefs, it is not likely he or she will consider alternative measures. Do you see how narrow and dangerous this kind of thinking can become without intervention?

The cognitive distortions during secondary appraisal can lead to various negative emotions unless you catch the distortions before they have a chance to reinforce your negative core beliefs. A dentist would say it's like removing plaque from your teeth before it turns into tartar. The cognitive distortions are the "plaque," and the negative core beliefs are the "tartar," with tartar being the more difficult to remove from your teeth than plaque.

Can you change core beliefs?

The negative core beliefs you formed as a child shape your view of the world. They begin to color every thought you have about yourself and your relation to the world. You look at things through a "false lens" that makes you see things inaccurately. Once this happens, it's difficult to examine your distorted cognitions with an open mind, let alone attempt to challenge your core beliefs. For most adults, once core beliefs emerge fully formed from childhood, they are difficult to challenge. But we have free will, which means we aren't deterministic machines. Unlike other animals, we have that capacity for self-reflection and critical thinking.

Perhaps part of the reason psychology is in the midst of a cognitive revolution when it comes to the implementation of CBT is because of our new knowledge about the brain (Schwartz 2003). It appears that the brain is malleable. Several decades ago, people thought children stopped forming new connections once they reached a certain age. Using that logic, a child's core beliefs were fixed for life. But today we know that's not entirely true. The brain is "plastic", and never stops forming new synapses or neurological connections. While most of the connections are formed in early childhood, when the brain is still in its most receptive stage (explaining why it's easier for a child to learn a new language than an adult), the truth is that connections never stop forming. The brain's neuroplasticity allows it to form new connections, negating the fallacy, "You can't teach an old dog (or human) new tricks." In fact, you can. This means it is possible to reverse long held, maladaptive beliefs and attitudes. The human brain never stops rewiring itself. This is powerful scientific knowledge that applies to our cognitive lives as well. We can always "retrain" our brains to shed outdated beliefs and modes of behavior and substitute new ones in their place.

Cost-benefit analysis

Let's say you have evaluated some of your negative core beliefs and no matter how hard you try to challenge them during secondary appraisal, you still believe they're true. In all likelihood, this is bound to happen. After all, you have been holding on to many of these beliefs since childhood, so they're not going to disappear without a fight. Assuming all else failed and you couldn't talk yourself out of the belief, I would advise you to ask yourself two key questions based on the advice of Burns (1980):

1. How does keeping this negative belief benefit me?

2. What is the personal (emotional) cost associated with keeping this negative belief?

Some beliefs, no matter their perceived truth, are self-destructive and produce negative consequences and aren't worth keeping. Burns (1980) suggests performing a cost-benefit analysis on such beliefs. Let's put it to the test with this prevalent core belief among people with Asperger's:

> The world is unfair to people with disabilities and, specifically, those with Asperger's.

You may truly believe this and not attribute it as a by-product of a cognitive distortion, even after intense analysis. That being the case, ask yourself how hanging on to this negative belief will benefit you in any way. The answer is it won't benefit you, unless you're going to take action toward improving the situation that currently exists for people with Asperger's, and, in turn, improving your own situation. If you took action, maybe this core belief would benefit you by justifying your action. On the other hand, what would it cost you to hang on to this negative core belief if you didn't do anything except complain about it? You would continue to resent the world, you may not want to interact with people due to mistrust, and you might feel anxious about living in a world that is unfair to people with disabilities.

Another strategy is to imagine the resulting emotions from hanging on to a particular belief. In the case of the world's unfair treatment of people with disabilities, there are a couple of scenarios. If dissatisfaction spurred you into action, you would probably feel empowered, optimistic, and altruistic, but if you held on to the core negative belief and took no action other than to vent and complain, you would end up feeling disempowered, depressed, anxious, and angry.

Here's the main point on the cost-benefit analysis: It's okay to give yourself permission to discard a negative core belief you might even believe to be true, especially if you feel the belief won't serve your best interests. It's not worth the energy you expend on it. If you try this approach, you'll notice long-held beliefs will melt away, and you will come to realize their meaninglessness.

Reviewing this section about cost-benefit analysis, keep in mind the two key questions when determining the value of a belief:

1. How does keeping this negative belief benefit me?

2. What is the personal (emotional) cost associated with keeping this negative belief?

Schemas

The term "core beliefs" comes from a psychological concept called *schemas,* coined by developmental psychologist Jean Piaget (Singer and Revenson 1979) in the 1920s. In Piaget's way of thinking, a schema is a mental representation that helps us organize our world so it makes sense to us. We use schemas all the time. They include stereotypes, rules of social understanding, thoughts about your own self-concept and worldviews. Sometimes though, schemas can make us inflexible when we receive a new piece of information that doesn't seem to fit within our current worldview. We automatically tend to filter out that information, with minimal, if any, conscious thought about it. We do this so our schema remains intact. Psychologists call this proactive interference (Goldstein 2007). We have been speaking of proactive interference throughout most of this chapter without labeling it as such. Proactive interference occurs when, during secondary appraisal, you are not open to reframing a cognitive distortion or revising a core belief, or schema. Either you ignore it completely, or you must incorporate the new information as part of your current worldview. Those are the two basic choices.

When you incorporate the new information, Piaget would say you are using the process of assimilation (Singer and Revenson 1979). For example, if you saw only black Labrador retrievers as a child, and suddenly you saw a golden retriever, assimilation would enable you to recognize the golden retriever is also a dog. Your core belief, "All dogs are black," capitulates, based on your new information. Further, recognizing the golden retriever as a different type of dog, you would be doing what Piaget calls accommodating (accommodation), as you developed an entirely new schema beyond "dog".

In this chapter we have been looking closely at self-schemas, beliefs that focus around your own self-concept. As previously mentioned, there is an offshoot of CBT that uses self-schemas as its focal point. Not surprisingly, it is called *schema therapy*.

Schema therapy

Jeffrey Young, a colleague of CBT practitioner Aaron Beck, developed schema therapy. In Beck-style CBT, the therapist is not particularly concerned with a client's past. He or she wants to focus on your current thought processes and ways to change current maladaptive beliefs. What this approach misses (in my opinion) is how these thoughts or beliefs were formed in the first place. CBT is useful when it comes to identifying and changing maladaptive thoughts, but often it is hard to do so without understanding the origins of those thoughts and beliefs. That's how schema therapy is different.

Jeffery Young (Klosko, Weishaar and Young 2006) felt Beck's approach of treating current beliefs was too limiting. According to Young, to get at the root of the problem, one has to understand the formation of those beliefs. This is key to schema therapy. Once a person has that understanding, he or she is ready cognitively to reframe outdated beliefs. According to Young, most of our early maladaptive schemas (EMS) are formed in childhood. Without intervention or self-examination, our EMS becomes part of who we are.

Early maladaptive schemas and how they relate to Asperger's

We've spent most of the chapter talking about negative core beliefs, but until now we haven't explored the different types of these core beliefs. In this section, I will explain how I think many of these core beliefs were formed, taking into account the impact of Asperger syndrome on these beliefs.

As is true for neurotypicals, not everyone with Asperger's will present all these negative core beliefs or EMS. I am highlighting how it is possible for a particular core belief to have formed for someone with Asperger syndrome. Young (Klosko, Weishaar and Young 2006) states there are five domains containing 18 EMS/negative core beliefs. For a review of all 18, refer to Young and Klosko in the bibliography.

I have paraphrased the five domains as follows:

1. **Disconnection and rejection:** People who have EMS/negative core beliefs in this domain don't trust the world. Their underlying negative core belief is the world is not a safe place. For people with Asperger's, beliefs from this domain might have developed as a result of teachers and parents not understanding their needs, being bullied, and not being able to count on people's support in childhood (Carley 2008).

2. **Impaired autonomy and performance:** People with EMS/ negative core beliefs in this domain don't feel secure in their ability to function independently or survive without some outside support. Their underlying negative core belief is they cannot function adequately in the world. For people with Asperger's, beliefs from this domain might have developed as a result of feeling socially incompetent in school and having problems with executive functioning such as organizing and making decisions. Parents might have also contributed to these beliefs if they did not understand their child's neurological difference and blamed

the child for his or her actions, thinking the deficiency was a type of personality disorder rather than a neurological disorder.

3. **Impaired limits:** People with EMS/negative core beliefs in this domain generally have low frustration tolerance when it comes to achieving self-set goals or being patient with others. They believe if something can't be perfect, it is unacceptable. Their underlying negative core belief is things are either good or bad. For people with Asperger's, beliefs from this domain might have developed because of the perfectionism that seems to be an inherent part of the syndrome, as well as challenges with emotional regulation and impulse control.

4. **Other directedness:** People with EMS/negative core beliefs in this domain believe without other people's approval, they are worthless. Their underlying negative core belief is they are worthless without the approval of others. For people with Asperger's, beliefs from this domain might have developed because of the constant disapproval we experienced as children. To make the world seem like a safer place, we try to please others.

5. **Over-vigilance and inhibition:** People with EMS/negative core beliefs in this domain feel they are out of control and something could go wrong at any moment. This creates an inhibited way of interacting with the world. Their underlying negative core belief is the world is a scary, unsafe place. For people with Asperger's, beliefs from this domain might have developed because of receiving punishment for our childhood meltdowns and mistakes.

I am hypothesizing most of your negative core beliefs stem from these five statements:

1. People cannot be trusted.

2. I cannot function adequately in the world.

3. Things are either good or bad.

4. I am inherently worthless/I have worth only when I have the approval of others.

5. The world is unpredictable and unsafe.

Carefully consider each of these statements and see how many of your negative core beliefs relate to them.

Let's take a more detailed look at each of the domains from the work of Jeffery Young and examine the beliefs most relevant to our population that fall under all five domains. Even though I write in terms of "us" and "we," please realize that not everything in the forthcoming list will apply to you.

1. Disconnection and rejection/the world is not a safe place

Abandonment/instability

This EMS occurs when a person mistrusts other people for fear of abandonment. This core belief creates anxiety for a person because the individual believes forming relationships isn't a safe thing to do. It's possible the abandonment schema came about when we felt abandoned by teachers who didn't understand our needs, or if parents or siblings became emotionally distant because they didn't understand our behavioral differences. Perhaps siblings felt we were getting too much attention and they became resentful. This happened between my cousin who has Asperger's and his neurotypical younger brother. The younger brother resented that his older brother received so much more attention than he did, and it affected their relationship negatively growing up. As adults, they have reconciled and now have a terrific relationship. I've also met many individuals with Asperger's who tell me they feel like the world turned its back on them when they were children; people were too quick to make negative judgments and disregard them. By middle school, there was less structure in place for our peer relationships, and many of us felt abandoned by our peers.

Mistrust

Someone with this EMS/core belief fears others will take advantage of him. Anxiety develops from this belief because the individual always feels like he is a potential victim for people with ill intentions. This schema could have easily developed for the child with Asperger's when due to his naïve nature, people played tricks or pranks on him. Clearly, the bullying we experienced as children instilled within us a certain amount of cynicism toward others. We tend to be a trusting and gullible group (Dubin 2007) making us easy targets for bullies. As an adult person with Asperger's, it makes sense that to protect ourselves, we change from being overly trusting to being less trusting and more cynical of others.

Emotional deprivation

This EMS/core belief arises when you realize your emotional needs will not be met by others and you must take sole responsibility for meeting your own needs. The anxiety that develops with this EMS is because of a fear of "being burned". In response to that fear, you tend to distance yourself emotionally from others. Often as children, we did not establish the same connections to the social world as our neurotypical counterparts. As a result, we had to fend for ourselves. To some extent, it might explain why some of us could have formed this core belief, not having experienced the same level of friendship or intimacy with peers during childhood and adolescence. We might decide we have to meet our own emotional needs since others are not reliable or trustworthy.

Social isolation/alienation

This EMS/core belief forms when we believe we're different from others and don't fit in socially. A type of existential anxiety develops with this EMS because we feel like fish out of water. It's easy to see how this particular EMS/core belief could have formed for a person with Asperger's. All of our lives, we have known we are different. We've had it reflected in other people's reaction to us. This may explain why many people with Asperger's experience relief upon getting their diagnosis later in life. Essentially, they feel they are suddenly part of a community of people (maybe for the first time in their lives), and the feeling of social isolation and alienation lessens (Carley 2008). But for undiagnosed adults who do not have a schizoid personality, social isolation is a major problem. These adults see themselves as being freaks, outcasts, and troublemakers. If only they knew how many "freaks and geeks" (to borrow from Asperger's author Luke Jackson 2002) without Asperger's existed, they would feel much better about themselves.

Failure to achieve

This EMS/core belief refers to a person feeling more inadequate than his or her peers. In our competitive society, anxiety develops when one uses the accomplishments of others as a yardstick for his or her level of success. Did we fail to achieve in any areas of our lives? In certain ways, no. Many people with Asperger's are known for their academic accomplishments. Perhaps you excelled in certain subjects in school. Where most of us have failed to achieve, however, is in the realm of social relationships. We saw our peers dating while we stood on the sidelines. Many of us didn't go to a high school prom and didn't receive invitations to parties. If you weren't diagnosed with Asperger's or never heard of it, you might ask yourself, "What is it that makes me socially less desirable than someone else?" Many of us have also experienced trouble in the workplace. This, I believe, is a core belief that forms later in life. After years of frustration in the workplace, we begin to view ourselves as failures. In the anxiety that arises from this belief, we become petrified to fail because it has been a repeated pattern throughout our lives.

2. Impaired autonomy and performance/I cannot function adequately in the world

Dependence/incompetence

This EMS/negative core belief forms when a person doesn't believe she can handle the responsibilities of being an adult. The anxiety that can develop from this EMS is the person may believe she is helpless in the world and cannot take care of herself. For the person with Asperger's, this belief might have formed as a reaction to the overwhelming nature of daily life. We might have been too dependent on our caretakers to help or assist us manage our lives due to our poor executive functioning abilities. Many people with Asperger's live at home well into adulthood. A person may have become so dependent on caregivers (usually parents), she truly believes she doesn't have the ability or stamina to be a self-sufficient adult.

Vulnerability to harm and illness

This EMS/negative core belief stems from when we feel a potential catastrophe is bound to happen at any minute. As a result, we become hypervigilant. This is pervasive for people with Asperger's. Many of us are not comfortable with changing circumstances or challenges with an unknown outcome. Yet that is how life works. It's unpredictable. Many people I have met with Asperger's feel something bad is about to happen. Perhaps as a child, you became hyper-vigilant toward protecting yourself from an ever-dangerous world, with all of its changes, challenges, and difficulties. Perhaps you found it necessary to be hyper-vigilant because as you saw it an impeding crisis was always lurking. Teachers may have berated you for your unusual learning style. A parent might have lambasted you for your disorganization. Schoolmates often ignored you. Soon, you simply expected bad things to happen because they had happened so many times in the past.

Enmeshment/undeveloped self

In essence, people with this EMS/negative core belief lack a sense of self. For individuals with Asperger's, this belief might have formed because of the rejection we experienced as children. The constant rejection could explain many of us rejecting ourselves. Because other people couldn't accept us for who we were, we didn't accept ourselves. This difficulty of developing an identity could then lead one to experiencing an existential crisis. We might have developed enmeshment with caretakers who tried to protect us from the harsh realities of the world, since they sensed we were so vulnerable. However, many people with Asperger's have not developed this core belief. They are entirely individualistic and prefer to stay that way. They aren't enmeshed with anyone. Their self-esteem is healthy, if not bordering on arrogance. Their positive core belief is, "I am proud of my individuality."

3. Impaired limits/things are either good or bad

Insufficient self-control/low frustration tolerance

The core belief that can develop when one has low frustration tolerance is, "Things must be perfect all the time." Or, "I either do a perfect job on something or it's lousy. There is no in-between."

4. Other directness/I am worthless (or) I am worthless without the approval of others
Subjugation

This EMS/core belief arises when we feel the need to acquiesce to the needs of others. The anxiety that arises with this EMS is we fear people will reject us if we don't do exactly what they want us to do. This may have arisen when we were children and couldn't follow or understand the *hidden curriculum* that everyone else seemed to understand intuitively. The hidden curriculum talked about by Brenda Smith-Myles (Schelvan, Smith-Myles and Trautman 2004) comprises the tacit rules that govern social settings. People assume, without you having received direct instruction, you know the social cues. Part of a hidden social curriculum at school could be never to wear Velcro shoes once you reached middle school, but of course, some of us with Asperger's never understood that social cue. As adults, we became hyper-vigilant to try our best to make sure we understand and comply with all the unwritten rules.

5. Over-vigilance and inhibition/the world is unpredictable
Over-control/emotional inhibition

For people with this EMS/negative core belief, the fear is expressing their emotions will lead to trouble. Consequently, they inhibit themselves and remain stoic, fearing if they display their emotions too strongly, the world will turn against them. As children, many of us were easily overwhelmed from an emotional or sensory standpoint. Unlike many children who could rein in their emotions and release them at a more opportune time, we had public meltdowns. We were told these emotional releases were bad, disruptive, excessive, and out of control. We were punished for our outbursts. After a while, we learned the world does tolerate strong emotional outbursts, so we generalized this lesson and became emotionally inhibited. I do not believe the adage that people with Asperger's have fewer emotions than neurotypicals. If anything, I think our emotional range is greater and more intense. When we release an emotion, it might be likened to a volcano exploding.

What I hoped to do in this section was to help you understand how having Asperger Syndrome has influenced some of your negative core beliefs. Not everything we have discussed will apply to you. However, I would expect much of this information will resonate with most of you. If you can recognize how and why your EMS/negative core beliefs formed, you can recognize when these beliefs are wreaking havoc in your life.

The exciting news from this chapter is you have a choice. From the research on brain neuroplasticity to the exciting successes of CBT, we know people have the power to overcome and transform even the most ingrained negative beliefs. The choice is yours. You can continue to be plagued from events that occurred in childhood, or you can view them as outdated beliefs that need updating.

Putting it all together

Let's revisit some of the earlier examples I gave regarding the cognitive distortions from the beginning of the chapter and see how they relate to the five core statements and the EMS.

1. Jenny's *all or nothing* thinking that she can never cook a bad meal reinforces these core beliefs:

- Things are either good or are bad.

- I am worthless.

The EMS it reinforces are:

- Failure to achieve (I am a failure).

- Vulnerability to harm (Something bad is bound to happen. I am going to cook another bad meal).

- Low frustration tolerance (Things must be perfect all of the time).

2. Nick *disqualifying the positive* feedback he got on his speeches reinforces these core beliefs:

- Things are either good or are bad.

- I am worthless.

- I am worthless without the approval of others.

- I cannot function adequately in this world.

The EMS it reinforces are:

- Abandonment (Perhaps no one will invite me to speak anymore).

- Failure to achieve (I am worthless as a speaker).

- Low frustration tolerance (I can't handle getting bad reviews on my speeches).

- Subjugation (I will have to try to please everyone so no one will reject me as a speaker).

3. Daryl's *fortune telling* error that no one will ever go on a second date with him reinforces these core beliefs:

- People can't be trusted (I can't trust my next date).

- I can't function adequately in the world (Anyone who is single is a loser. Therefore, I'm a loser with no place in this world).

- I am worthless.

- The world is unpredictable (Who needs dating? It's too unpredictable).

The EMS it reinforces are:

- Abandonment and instability (I am bound to be abandoned if I continue dating, or I am bound to be abandoned if I get too close to someone who then rejects me).

- Mistrust (I've been taken advantage of too many times in my life. I don't trust people enough to want to become intimate with them. I need to keep my distance).

- Emotional deprivation (My emotional needs cannot be met by others, only myself. Therefore, dating doesn't have anything to offer me).

- Social isolation/feeling different (I am clearly a freak. Why would anyone want to date me?)

- Failure to achieve (Look at me! I can't even get a girlfriend. How pathetic is that?)

- Incompetence (I can't handle the responsibilities of being in a relationship).

- Vulnerability to harm (I don't want to get hurt again).

- Undeveloped self (I don't feel I have enough of a self-identity to be able to share my life with another person).

- Low frustration tolerance (The ups and downs a romantic relationship brings would be too much for me to handle).

4. Professor Wilkinson's *personalization* error that he is not getting through to his students because many of them didn't turn in a homework assignment on a particular day reinforces these core beliefs:

- I am worthless

- Things are either good or bad (Either my students turn in their homework all of the time, or I am not getting through to them).

The EMS it reinforces are:

- Failure to achieve (I must be doing a terrible job since my students have been lazy with their homework assignment).

- Undeveloped self (My identity revolves around being a good professor. Whenever I feel I am ineffective, it diminishes my identity).

- Low frustration tolerance (I demand perfection from myself and others and can't tolerate anything less).

I hope you can see how closely intertwined our beliefs, schemas, and cognitive distortions are. The point of this chapter is this: When you view the world inaccurately, it creates an inordinate amount of unnecessary anxiety you can avoid. The focus of the rest of this book will be on understanding how you, as an individual with Asperger's, experience the world and what distortions, core beliefs and schemas you have.

There are legitimate concerns for you to be anxious about. I don't want you to think I am undermining your issues and fears. There are very real factors that make living with Asperger's an unpredictable and sometimes unnerving experience. I don't think anyone will deny that point, but with life as unpredictable and scary as it is, do you really want to magnify these obstacles and challenges even more so? If you can learn to assimilate and then accommodate more positive and realistic schemas into your overall view, your life will be less anxiety-filled than it is today.

Let's review this challenging chapter:

Action points

- Reframing your thoughts means consciously slowly down and examining your old thoughts to determine whether they are logical. If they aren't logical, replace them with thoughts that are.

- Create a cost-benefit ratio regarding your thoughts. Ask yourself if there's more cost or benefit when it comes to holding onto certain thoughts? Be realistic.

- Think about where and why some of your core beliefs may have formed and make way for a more updated belief system.

- To create new core beliefs or schemas, create a list of positive affirmations about yourself and reaffirm those affirmations on a daily basis, until you really believe them.

- Learn and practice the skills from this chapter—you will be much less anxious and more in control of your emotions.

Chapter 4

Mindfulness

In this chapter I'd like to elaborate on the concept of schemas and discuss ways to become mindful of them. I will teach you the benefits of keeping your consciousness focused on the present. One of those benefits is to increase mindfulness.

To become mindful is to actively become the "computer programmer" of your own mind. Mindfulness means to quietly "observe" your thought patterns. In doing so, you will control your mind rather than the other way around. Mindfulness is highly valued and appreciated among Buddhist cultures as well as spiritual practitioners throughout the world.

Going back to secondary appraisal, you will recall that we carefully examine what happened during the fight-or-flight situation to determine whether our thoughts truly do match up with reality. In Chapter 3, we noted secondary appraisal loses its value if the cognitive distortions and early maladaptive schemas are so strong they don't allow a re-evaluation of the situation to take place. Going forward, we will focus on secondary appraisal and ways to disengage from unhealthy thoughts before or after a stressful situation.

Schema attack

It's important to understand each of the schemas in the last chapter have their own distinct emotional flavor (Goleman 2001). Each of the schemas makes us anxious about something unique to that schema, although there is naturally some overlap between the schemas. The first step in dismantling an early maladaptive schema (EMS) is to be aware of it before it activates. A schema attack occurs when one of these EMS becomes fully activated in your psyche. Schemas are always present to some degree, but when fully emerged in consciousness, they exert the most power over you. When this happens, your view of reality is likely to become narrower and more distorted. In this chapter, I will correlate each of these schemas with the distinct emotional triggers that accompany them.

Abandonment/instability

This EMS occurs when a person mistrusts others for fear of abandonment. This core belief creates anxiety because the individual believes forming relationships isn't a safe thing to do.

Emotions this EMS will likely trigger:

1. An exaggerated anxiety toward loss.

2. An almost overwhelming fear of isolation.

3. An increased fear of rejection.

Pay attention to situations in which:

1. Someone doesn't immediately return a phone call.

2. Friends or significant others don't respond promptly to your needs.

Mistrust

Someone with this EMS/core belief has the constant fear he is being taken advantage of. Anxiety develops because the individual feels like he is a potential victim for others with ill intentions.

Emotions this EMS will likely trigger:

1. Fear of being engulfed by others and having your space invaded.

2. Fear of the world.

3. Fear of being unintelligent.

Pay attention to situations in which:

1. You feel exaggeratedly suspicious toward others.

2. You feel the need to be overly trusting to prove to yourself you aren't suspicious of the world (Klosko, Weishaar and Young 2006). This could be the schema manifesting itself in an unconscious fashion.

Emotional deprivation

The EMS/core belief arises when a person realizes her emotional needs cannot be met by others and only by herself.

Emotions this EMS will likely trigger:

1. Fear of losing your identity to another person.

2. Fear of being engulfed by others.

3. Fear of or anger from unmet expectations from others, leading to sadness and loss.

Pay attention to situations where:

1. Your expectations of others are unrealistic.

2. You become overly sensitive to criticism.

Social isolation/alienation

This EMS/core belief forms when the person believes he is different and doesn't fit in.

Emotions this EMS will likely trigger:

1. A fear of defectiveness.

2. A fear of inadequacy.

3. A fear of rejection.

Pay attention to situations in which:

1. You are overly worried someone may view you negatively.

2. You notice you begin withholding the opportunity for social interaction for fear of rejection.

Failure to achieve

This EMS/core belief commonly refers to a person who feels more inadequate than his or her peers.

Emotions this EMS will likely trigger:

1. A fear of incompetence.

2. A fear of being useless.

3. A fear of not finding a place in the world.

Pay attention to situations in which:

1. You excessively compare yourself to others.

2. You find you are overly harsh on yourself when you make a mistake or do something less than perfect.

Dependence/incompetence

This EMS/core belief forms when a person doesn't believe she can handle the responsibilities of adulthood.

Emotions this EMS will likely trigger:

1. A fear of incompetence.

2. A fear of independence.

3. A fear of being unable to meet the responsibilities of life.

Pay attention to situations in which:

1. You find yourself depending on others for help with tasks you are fully capable of doing.

2. You find yourself reluctant to move out of your parents' house.

Vulnerability to harm and illness

This EMS/core belief occurs when we feel a potential catastrophe is bound to happen. As a result, we become hyper-vigilant.

Emotions this EMS will likely trigger:

1. A fear of the unknown.

2. A fear of potential catastrophic events.

3. A fear of getting sick and dying.

Pay attention to situations in which:

1. You experience generalized anxiety and begin to worry about everything.

2. You fixate on death and constantly think it could happen at any time.

Enmeshment/undeveloped self

People with this EMS/negative core belief lack a sense of self.
Emotions this EMS will likely trigger:

1. A fear of lacking an identity.

2. A fear of becoming autonomous.

Pay attention to situations in which:

1. You feel an unusually strong emotional connection to someone and never want to leave that person.

2. Your sense of identity derives itself from a relationship with one or more close individuals.

Insufficient self-control/low frustration tolerance

Everything must be "perfect" all of the time.
Emotions this EMS will likely trigger:

1. A fear of ambiguity.

2. A fear of not being perfect.

Pay attention to situations in which:

1. You sense something isn't black and white but instead, involves shades of grey and this makes you anxious.

2. You have constant meltdowns.

Subjugation

This EMS/core belief arises when we feel the need to acquiesce to the needs of others.

Emotions this EMS will likely trigger:

1. A fear of losing other's approval.

2. A fear of being abused if you don't do exactly what you are told.

Pay attention to situations in which:

1. You fear disapproval.

2. You act against your inner convictions and do things people want you to do for fear of losing their approval.

Overcontrol/emotional inhibition

The fear for people with this EMS/negative core belief is expressing their emotions will get them into trouble.

Emotions this EMS will likely trigger:

1. A fear of being out of control emotionally, i.e., obsessively worrying about when the next meltdown will occur.

2. A fear of being out of control in general.

Pay attention to situations in which:

1. You hold back your emotions to the point of feeling numb inside.

2. You are afraid to confront someone for fear of overreacting.

I suggest spending some time reviewing this section until you have a fairly good idea what your triggers may be. You'll be surprised how easy it is to control your reactions to stressful situations once you become aware of those triggers and how they impact you. Once you shed outdated core beliefs and refine early maladaptive schemas, you will be another step closer to lowering your anxiety level on a daily basis.

For a more detailed and comprehensive discussion on schemas and how they work, I suggest reading *Emotional Alchemy* (Goleman 2001).

Present moment awareness

One shortcut to becoming mindful is to try to keep focused on the present moment, the "now". This practice, around for centuries, has recently resurfaced in popular culture thanks to a German mystic named Eckhart Tolle (1999). Tolle wrote a book called *The Power of Now,* in which he advocated one should mentally strive to focus on the present moment; not on the past or the future.

This seems to be an easy concept to grasp but difficult to put into practice. Having Asperger's makes the utilization of this skill even more challenging. Because we are often adrift in social situations, we tend to spend a lot of time analyzing them after they occur. Additionally, our difficulty socializing makes us highly anxious and produces an anticipatory fear before we actually interact with people. I've met many individuals with Asperger's who have difficulty falling asleep because they can't stop thinking about how they could have acted differently in certain social situations that day or week.

There is a mental benefit for staying in the present. Think about an activity you particularly enjoy doing. It could be flying a kite, looking at maps, driving or any activity that brings joy to your life. When you are involved in that activity, you aren't thinking about anything else. You focus all your attention on what you are doing. Your focus allows you to enjoy that activity. During these moments of bliss, you aren't thinking about paying bills, running errands, or upcoming social obligations. The only thing you are focused on is the activity itself. When a person is involved in a creative pursuit, this concept is known as being "in the flow". You lose track of time while caught up in the activity.

Imagine being in that state of mind in everyday life. It's easier to be in the present when you're doing something you enjoy. It's more challenging to be in this state of mind when you are fearful, anxious, or bored. Nevertheless, it is a state of mind that can effectively help to reduce anxiety even when you're not involved in a joyful activity.

Let me give you an example: I used to play tennis competitively. I was the number one singles player on my high school and college tennis teams. I was also a highly ranked player in my five-state tournament region and played against some of the top players of the region. I remember both the matches in which I performed well and those in which I didn't. When I wasn't playing well, I was usually worrying about the consequences of what would happen if I lost the match. Would my high school team-mates be mad at me or disappointed? Would I drop down within the ranking system? Would people view me as a failure? Could I beat an opponent who had consistently beaten me in the past? Would my coach lose respect for me?

Whenever I was on the tennis court and obsessing about these types of questions, I would lose 99 per cent of the time. On the other hand, when I just focused on winning one point at a time, I won more often than I lost. Tennis is a great metaphor for life. When you are fully engaged in the present moment, you will perform better, no matter the activity. Why? Because you are not experiencing anxiety and stress from worrying about past events or future consequences.

It doesn't make sense to dwell on the past or fixate on the future. You can't change the past and the future depends on what you do in the present. It's possible to become so concerned with the future you sabotage yourself in the present and paradoxically, you adversely affect the future. When you stay focused in the present, you actually bring about a better future. As a tennis player, if I worried about whether I was going to win or lose the match, I almost always lost. Worrying about the future caused me to suffer the very consequences I was worrying about. However, when I let go of expectations and immersed myself in a match, I performed better and won more often. My worrying was self-defeating.

Our experience of life is in the present. Once it is gone, we are then into the next moment. You can never re-gain the time you spend worrying about the past or future. Make the most of every moment.

The other benefit of present moment awareness is it reduces the number of things you worry about. Most of our worries stem from the "perceived past" or the "feared future", to quote one of my best psychology professors that I had in college, Dr. Bruce Hillenberg. In the present moment, we deal with whatever confronts our attention. The process of worrying is usually reserved for a time before or after the moment in question. In the here and now, there is usually nothing to worry about, save some immediate threat. For instance, if your house is on fire or the landlord is trying to evict you, these are present moment worries. The anxieties these situations generate are real and need to be addressed. The majority of the time, though, thoughts that induce stress and anxiety in life are not usually happening. Rather, we are anticipating or replaying events that are not in real time. The key to becoming mindful is to be fully aware when your mind is drifting away from the present moment.

This attitude does not mean you should be apathetic and unconcerned about the future. If the landlord comes to evict you, it probably means you did not take care of your rental responsibilities. The difference between worrying about being evicted and doing something to prevent it is important to note. Worrying about eviction is to focus exclusively on the future. Taking action to prevent eviction is engaging in the present to bring about a favorable result in the future. If you are evicted, despite your best efforts, all the worrying in the world wouldn't have helped your cause. It's just wasted energy giving rise to unnecessary anxiety.

Going with the flow

Individuals with Asperger's may have an inherent advantage over most neurotypicals when it comes to being mindful. In 1991, human potential psychologist, Miahly Csikzentmihalyi, wrote a groundbreaking book that tried to encapsulate the qualities needed to achieve a "flow" state. He aptly titled his 1991 book *Flow*.

What is a flow state? It is similar to what athletes call "being in the zone," where you can seemingly do no wrong. Perhaps you were in a play back in high school and gave the performance of a lifetime. If so, you were in the flow state. Perhaps you wrote a brilliant poem that received first prize in a writing competition. If so, you were in the flow state while writing the poem. Perhaps you gave a speech at a conference and felt as if everything that came out of your mouth was stated in the best possible manner; you weren't capable of missing a single point. Again, this would be the flow state.

Csikzentmihalyi (1991) described a number of characteristics that typify this wonderful state of being. I will paraphrase them for you:

1. **Clear goals:** expectations and rules are discernible; goals are attainable and align appropriately with one's skill set and abilities.

2. **Concentrating and focusing:** a high degree of concentration within a limited field (the person engaged in the activity will have the opportunity to focus and delve deeply).

3. **A loss of self-consciousness:** the merging of action and awareness.

4. **Distorted sense of time:** one's subjective experience of time is altered.

5. **Direct and immediate feedback:** successes and failures in the course of the activity are apparent, and behavior adjusts accordingly.

6. **Balance between ability level and challenge:** the activity is neither too easy nor too difficult.

7. **A sense of personal control over the situation or activity.**

8. **Intrinsic rewards:** motivation and action are effortless.

9. **Action awareness merging:** people become so absorbed in their activity the focus is narrowed down to the activity itself. (Csikszentmihalyi, 1991)

It's amazing to realize that many of these "flow" characteristics are in evidence among people with Asperger syndrome. Are you able to identify with some of them? Small wonder why so many creative geniuses are thought to have Asperger's. To be engaged in this kind of creative flow requires a certain amount of mindfulness at the outset. When a person is in the flow state, he or she taps into the present and is fully engaged in whatever the activity. We "Aspies" are inherently good at achieving a flow state. Yet, we are also inherently anxious. This seems contradictory until you realize life—outside of our special interests—does not always make it easy for us to achieve the flow state. However, once we do achieve flow, it's very difficult to distract us.

Action points

- By becoming aware of your emotional triggers, you can become aware of your hot buttons and learn to relinquish outdated, early maladaptive schemas.

- By staying in the present, we actually perform better, no matter what the task. Stay in the present!

- Individuals with Asperger's have an inherent advantage focusing on things that interest us, but the realities of life do not always make that easy. Try to immerse yourself in your passions and generalize that feeling to the rest of your life!

Chapter 5

Anxiety and relationships

For many people with Asperger's, nothing conjures up more fear than the thought of a relationship. On the one hand, the overwhelming majority of individuals I have met with Asperger's would very much like to enter the dating scene and find a life partner. On the other hand, it scares the daylights out of most of us. This is understandable. Dating is a game, and unfortunately, many of us do not intuitively understand the rules of the game. Nevertheless, there are many reasons why I believe you can lower your anxiety level regarding dating and relationships by reframing a few significant core beliefs you probably have formed. First, I will share a few stories from my past about dating.

My dating history

I didn't begin dating until I was 24. At that time, the thought of going on a date was petrifying to me. I was very cognizant of the fact that I was entering the game late. While many of my peers probably had their first kiss around puberty, I never even dreamed a "first kiss" was possible for me. When I finally had enough nerve to take that all-important first step and go on a date, I was at a distinct disadvantage. I was a neophyte, with no prior experience.

Because I didn't feel comfortable asking someone I knew to go on a date, I did the next safest thing: I tried to get a date with a stranger via online dating. As I looked through the scores of profiles of the various women, I became more and more intimidated. All of them read something like this: "Looking for an outgoing and funny person." "Looking for someone with self-confidence." "Looking for someone who likes to party."

I wanted to find profiles that read: "Looking for an honest and sincere person." "Looking for someone who will be devoted and loyal." "Looking for a non-conformist."

It didn't matter how long I looked. All the women were seemingly looking for a certain type of man, and I didn't fit the bill. My strategy at this point was to look for women who shared some common interests with me. Before too long, I found someone who seemed perfect as far as I was concerned. She was an amateur jazz singer who sang with a big band, and she lived within close proximity to me. Jazz was and is one of my passions. The fact I had found someone who was a jazz singer was a miracle from the divine, as far as I was concerned. I viewed it as a positive sign that the universe was sending me. I had to take advantage of this opportunity.

My plan was to instant message the woman and start spouting off my knowledge of jazz. Within a few minutes, I bombarded her with questions about her favorite jazz artists, the styles of jazz she listened to, at what age she started singing, etc. Initially she seemed impressed with the passion I was displaying about our area of mutual interest, and somewhat to my surprise, I seemed to be doing fine over the Internet. So far, so good.

After a few weeks of chatting with her via instant messages, the next big step was to ask her out on a date. Not wanting to talk to her on the telephone (because I thought I might trip up), I decided to casually gauge the situation online and ask her if she would like to have dinner. To my delight, she accepted my invitation.

Not knowing what to do on a date, I did know at the very least, I was going to be the perfect gentleman. I went to a florist and bought her a big bouquet of roses to symbolize my affection for her. "What affection?" you might be asking. After all, I had never met the woman before. Good point. Maybe the flowers were to really show her that I was a gentleman.

I showed up with my big bouquet of flowers expecting her to wrap her arms around me and fall madly in love with me. Instead, I got a confused look that even I, as someone with Asperger's, could clearly recognize. "This doesn't make sense," I thought to myself. "I just did a nice thing for her and she looks uncomfortable." We sat through the awkward dinner attempting some forced conversation that never amounted to anything. This result was clearly not what I had anticipated. I thought our date would be a natural continuation of our online conversations, but it didn't work out that way.

Afterwards, I e-mailed her for a second date and never received a response. The rejection I experienced deeply wounded me and merely reinforced certain negative core beliefs about myself. But I'm not a quitter. I decided to pick myself, dust myself off, and try again with someone new.

The same pattern emerged again and again. I would meet a woman who shared my interests. I would begin showering her with kindness and affection, which was met with a lack of interest or lack of desire to continue to go out with me. This pattern was disconcerting. A few times, I even sabotaged myself. In some instances, I acted inappropriately when I didn't hear back from my date after a few days. I would call and berate my date for—what seemed to me—her display of rude behavior. You can imagine how the women didn't appreciate this display of emotion.

Eventually, I did find someone who seemed to want to continue seeing me on a regular basis. However, certain problems developed for me in this ongoing relationship. I didn't know how to read romantic cues. I remember going to a movie with this particular woman, and she put her hand on mine and began massaging it. While she reasonably might have expected some reciprocity of a physical nature in return, instead, I tightened the muscles of my body and pulled my hand away. Confused and probably hurt, she withdrew emotionally. Eventually, the relationship dissolved.

Am I in a relationship right now? No. However, I'm certain if I were to actively seek a partner, I would find one. For the moment, it has become less of a priority for me than my career, which has started to take off and requires a lot of energy.

I know many of you reading this book would very much like to meet your life partner. I also know that what might be holding you back is fear. This chapter will try to help you confront that fear so you can confidently enter the foray of dating, if that's your goal.

Positive qualities

You may not realize it, but as a person with Asperger's, you bring many desirable qualities to a relationship that many (if not most) women would find appealing. Time after time at conferences where I speak, I meet married couples in which one of the partners has Asperger's. What I generally hear from the "neurotypical" spouse is he/she values the following traits of their Asperger's mate:

1. Loyalty and devotion (it's nice to know your husband isn't going to cheat on you).

2. Honesty.

3. A non-conformist and original personality.

You'll note, these are exactly the kinds of qualities I did not see among the online dating profiles. And that's exactly the point. There are certain women who prefer these kinds of qualities than those generally mentioned in the context of online dating. Read Maxine Aston's (2003) *Asperger's in Love* if you need proof there are plenty of individuals with Asperger's in committed relationships, albeit with a bit of struggle and sacrifice for both parties involved (as is true in any relationship). If they can make it work, so can you.

Let's look at some common core beliefs that may be keeping you from dating or committing to a relationship. The following factors constitute a composite list of remarks I've heard from people with Asperger's over the last five years.

No one would ever want to marry me

This thought stems from the core belief that you view yourself as worthless. Imagine carrying this core belief with you into any new dating situation. Right at the outset, you would be setting yourself up for a self-fulfilling prophecy. Aside from being a nervous wreck, the anxiety would turn into apathy. You would most likely become disengaged from the dating process since, in your mind, failure is the inevitable outcome.

Remember our friend, Daryl? He was terrified of dating because of a number of unresolved, deep-seated, negative core beliefs. He felt he was worthless, that dating was too unpredictable, and this made him feel like a loser. He feared abandonment, being taken advantage of, not having the other person meet his emotional needs, his own incompetence, and not being able to handle the ups and downs of a relationship. His fear paralyzed him from meeting a new dating prospect. Eventually, he became apathetic and gave up.

"That's easy for you to say, Nick," you might be thinking. "Someone who is constantly rejected cannot help but think of himself as a failure." I would counter by challenging you to reframe your whole concept of rejection. From a cognitive point of view, let's think about this notion rationally. As a person with Asperger's who happens to fall outside of the norm when it comes to social behaviors, it's only natural you probably will experience more rejection than someone who enjoys and is emotionally comfortable in a social context. If you are a person who is not good at math, you might have to work a little harder than another person who gets good grades in math because it comes easy to him. Just because you may have poorer math skills than someone doesn't make you a less valuable person. It's likely you'll experience more social rejection if you are a "late bloomer" with some visible social discomfort that is readily apparent to others. That's to be expected.

The big challenge for you will be not to personalize this rejection. And that will depend precisely on how you frame the rejection. If the rejection merely confirms your own feelings of inadequacy, then it will serve to reinforce your fears, and eventually, it will lead to apathy. Think back to the "all or nothing" cognitive distortion from a previous chapter. If rejection serves as a way to intensify your anxiety, you are using all-or-nothing thinking. Your rationale is something like this, "If I am rejected more than the average person when it comes to dating, then I am a worthless person." This is irrational. You probably will be rejected more than the average person because you present yourself in a more unique manner—not bad or defective, but unique. What's important is to be honest with yourself. You are no less desirable than someone else who has more charisma. We just happen to live in a culture that glorifies extroverted, outgoing, funny, socially confident people. If you lived in a non-western culture that valued intelligence, sophistication, thoughtfulness or even quirkiness, then you would most likely be a sought-after and attractive person. Equating the amount of rejection you experience with your value as a person becomes a fallacy when you examine this belief from a rational point of view.

We may live in a culture that glorifies certain types of people, but not everyone conforms to the same cultural values. All it takes is for one special person to come along and love you for who you are and believe in your potential. Will it take relatively longer for you to meet someone special than it might be for a socially adept person? Probably. It's understandable you might want to be cautious, but don't let your inhibitions get the best of you and prevent you from attaining your goals.

If you have been unable to establish a meaningful relationship, try to take the pressure off yourself and simply enjoy the dating process. Giving up the anxiety will help you enjoy the experience of dating. Don't get caught up with expectations of what should or should not happen.

It's too late for me

For many adults with Asperger's, dating is a long and arduous journey that doesn't begin until adulthood, as it did for me. Many of us, however, end up believing because we haven't dated earlier in life, we will be clueless and at a disadvantage when it comes to dating. This is understandable, but irrational. Since it's a belief that would likely cause us anxiety about dating, it's a belief we should examine.

If we look at this belief using cognitive-behavioral therapy, we would conclude it is irrational. Why? Because late bloomers exist. They exist in every aspect of the human experience. In sports, for example, tennis great Big Bill Tilden didn't become the world champion until the age of 27 (Deford 1976). To put this in perspective, most professional players emerge as champions before they turn 20. Civil rights attorney Virgil Hawkins of Florida didn't become a lawyer until he was in his middle 70s (Dubin 1993). The artist Grandma Moses didn't start painting until her 70s, and that was to help her with her arthritis!

Another example is my father. In an unlikely career move, my dad, Larry, became a law professor when he was in his late 30s after a decade as a successful trial lawyer. As a child, my dad was shy (almost meek) and non-confrontational. His legal career was partly responsible for reshaping his personality. Today he's confident and assertive. He's in demand as a legal expert on local and national television, is frequently quoted in newspapers, magazines, and journals, and appears on national radio programs, all with professional aplomb.

With what we now know about the brain's ability to change, this isn't terribly surprising. We have the capacity to change.

Let's get more specific and examine how change applies to relationships. At a conference at which I was speaking, I met a man in his late 40s. He told me he did not begin dating until his early 40s. Today, he is a happily married man with two children. He isn't the only one I've met with Asperger's with this story. It is not an uncommon phenomenon.

Late bloomers are even more common among people with Asperger's. So the next time you think, "It's too late," think again. As cliché as it might sound, it never is too late. With the knowledge you've gained from this section, you should feel a little less anxious about the dating process. This isn't to say dating will suddenly be easy for you. Knowing others have blazed the trail and have succeeded in an area that holds interest to you, should give you some confidence.

Ways to meet people

To lessen your anxiety when it comes to dating, it will help to plan ahead and have concrete strategies for accomplishing your dating goals. If you do what I did and start dating without putting much thought into your actions, you will end up needlessly frustrated.

Here are two simple strategies that might be helpful:

Shared interests

Having met many couples in which one member is on the autism spectrum and one is neurotypical, I have observed one factor that brings these couples together: shared special interests. Anxiety naturally decreases when you know there will be common interests to spark your conversation and encourage sharing experiences. If you have nothing in common with another person, you will find it difficult to be with that person. Common interests serve as your foundation. You can meet people with similar interests through:

1. Online message boards, i.e., www.wrongplanet.net or www. aspiesforfreedom.com.

2. Reputable online dating services.

3. College clubs and organizations.

4. Asperger's/autism-related activities; i.e. conferences, national or regional meetings.

Online dating services

There are some pros and cons to this approach. Traditional online dating services provide little more than a picture and a descriptive paragraph. There are many unknown factors and the validity of the data remains a mystery until you actually meet the person (or at least talk on the phone). You may get an idealized image of someone online that shatters into a million pieces once you meet them. And vice versa: you may dismiss someone with what you perceive to be an unacceptable profile who would, in actuality, be a person worth getting to know. If you go on a date not knowing what you're getting yourself into, you will experience anxiety.

One way to circumvent this and reduce the anxiety associated with a blind date is to find dating services where you already know you and your date will have some significant common interests. If you would prefer to meet someone on the autism spectrum, there is an online dating service that currently fit the bill: www.aspieaffection.com

For the men reading this, the bad news is you will outnumber the women. For the women, the odds are in your favor. The good news for both sides is it only takes one person to make the right connection.

The idealized image

If you're a heterosexual male, you may have an expectation your date should look like Miss America. If so, you're a normal, testosterone-producing guy. However, this attitude can be self-defeating in the long run, since the importance you attach to appearance may limit the number of dates worthy of your consideration. You then may become anxious you'll never find the woman you have idealized for so long. Let me give you an example.

At a conference, I listened to a well-known Asperger's speaker (who is also a friend) talk about his experiences helping other "Aspies" start the dating process. He described one young man who had poor hygiene and wasn't experiencing successful dates. One day, my friend observed this young man interacting with a female who seemed to show some interest in him, but surprisingly, the young man seemingly rebuffed the flirtation. My friend was confused by his reaction, so he went over to this man and asked why he wasn't more willing to engage this woman in conversation. The man replied, "Physically, she wasn't my type. I prefer them 36-24-36." Because she did not fit his ideal, he lost an opportunity to meet a potential date. During his speech, my friend went on to say many of us become reliant on pornography as an alternative way of engaging in romantic relationships. While it may serve as an outlet, it can also generate unrealistic expectations about how a date should look. To be blunt, most people you meet will not be as attractive as the models and/or actors from movies or videos. It's important to realize this fact and let go of unrealistic expectations.

Action points

- Recognize that dating does not come naturally to many of us with Asperger's, leading to prolonged anxiety about being in a relationship.

- You may have formed some negative core beliefs about yourself that are currently hindering your ability to date successfully. Try to examine those core beliefs with some rational objectivity.

- Try to list all of the positive qualities you think you can bring to a relationship.

- Realize you are likely to possess some qualities some women will find desirable.

- Looking at rejection differently will lessen the anticipatory anxiety you may have about meeting others.

- The easiest way to lessen anxiety when going on a date is to try to meet individuals with whom you share some common interests.

- Online message boards can be an effective way to meet others with Asperger's.

Chapter 6

Anxiety and employment

The prospect of employment is daunting for many of us with Asperger's. Anxiety about work is very real. Although many people with Asperger's are highly intelligent, creative, and innovative individuals, we do face our share of challenges in the workplace. While it is not uncommon for someone with Asperger's to perform extremely well in college, that same person may not do as well when it comes to performance on the job. I learned that lesson the hard way, but I'm also convinced with the right strategies in place, those of us with Asperger's can succeed on the job. In this chapter, I will talk about anxiety-related issues people with Asperger's may face. Because good instructional books regarding strategies for finding and maintaining employment exist for the Asperger population, I will limit my concerns to employment issues that involve anxiety.

My employment story

This true story has many sad moments but has a happy ending…

My first job was as a tennis instructor. I was 17 years old and received an unexpected call from a tennis professional who used to give me lessons when I was a boy. Doug (not his real name) was enthusiastic about hiring me as a summer tennis pro at a prestigious country club in a posh Detroit suburb. Without much deliberation, I decided to take the job. My attitude toward this job was it was going to be a cakewalk. I would be able to hang out at tennis courts all day and play tennis when I wasn't teaching. I couldn't have been more wrong.

The job was a harrowing experience. For starters, Doug constantly used to make fun of the way I walked, calling me "The Waddler". What was more upsetting was he encouraged the children taking the lessons to do the same. I felt humiliated.

Doug also liked to play practical jokes on me. One time, Doug, along with encouraging the children, locked me in the men's room by holding the door shut and prevented me from leaving. This protracted nightmare felt like an eternity. When they finally opened the door and let me leave the bathroom, I rushed to my car and headed home, never to return to that club.

I worked at a number of different tennis clubs through the years and the same problems always seemed to arise. For one thing, I never felt I was establishing a true social connection with the members, even though I tried to go out of my way to be friendly. Small talk never came easily to me. The amount of socializing that was required for a tennis pro was beginning to take a psychological toll on my well-being. I couldn't keep up with the pace of seven or eight group lessons in a row. Each class drained me, and I needed more than the five minutes of the transition time that was allotted between lessons. I also found it difficult to teach groups of children. They were unpredictable and rambunctious. Although some kids took their tennis lessons seriously, many didn't, wasting my time and theirs. (This pattern was a preview of what I would experience a few years later as a student teacher.) I did learn, however, that multitasking was not one of my strengths.

Not factoring in the negative experiences of working with children in a bustling environment, I decided to become a special education teacher. In theory, this was a logical choice. After all, I had received special education services throughout my years as a public school student. I wanted to help those who might have had similar learning challenges.

As a master's degree student, I breezed through my course work, ultimately graduating from the University of Detroit Mercy magna cum laude. As a graduate student, I became interested in the subject of learning disabilities and had the notion I might have finally pinpointed the passion that was going to blossom into my future career. However, once I began student teaching, this notion was quickly disproved. I'd very much like to forget the experience, but will never be able to do so.

My conversations with individuals on the autism spectrum have revealed there are two different types of anxiety we experience relative to employment. There are what I refer to as "existential employment worries" and "practical employment worries", both with their own distinctions. Let's delve into these two categories:

Existential employment worries

From talking with people who have Asperger's, the research I've done as a doctoral student in psychology, as well as my own personal work experiences, I'm convinced most of us suffer from existential anxiety when faced with the prospect of work. Work represents a compromise of our individuality. Since most of us with Asperger's take pride in our individuality and view it as an important part of our self-esteem, 9 to 5 jobs tend to diminish our essential selves. Look around at the corporate world of the 21st century. You'll see uniforms, codes of conduct, and scripted customer service. Disposability is as rampant as ever. The message many of us receive as potential employees in the corporate environment is if we do not fit in (like a cog in a well-oiled machine), we can be easily replaced. This fear we have about losing our sense of identity is legitimate and real. It isn't a cognitive distortion. Conformity reaps rewards while individuality, often times, reaps pink slips.

Another part of existential anxiety is the amount of time that work often demands. Most people who work full time are expected to put in a 40-hour week. Although many people work longer hours or even hold two jobs, from an Asperger's point of view, the limited down time from work doesn't give us sufficient time to recharge our batteries. Not only are many of us forced to try and play inauthentic roles while at work, we fear those roles will consume our real identity. After a while, we begin to lose touch with who we really are because we have become so accustomed to the energy it takes to get used to our work role. It's almost as if we don't know whether we are truly our work personas or ourselves. In other words, we transform into our work role beyond working hours, because changing personas from one setting to another takes too much energy for us. For those individuals with Asperger's who are married and have children, this becomes an even more complicated issue.

Burnout for both "Aspies" and neurotypicals is a real phenomenon. According to Paul Stiles (2006), author of *Is the American Dream Killing You*, Americans added five more weeks to their employment time from 1973 to 2000. Stiles also notes the phrase "time poverty" has come into vogue, which means people have less leisure time than ever before. Additionally, Stiles says our society has become much more competitive in the last few decades, both in business and socially (this hints at "practical employment worries," which we will be discussing shortly).

I suffer from existential worries. The thought of being forced to play out a certain role in the workplace for eight hours a day is utterly terrifying. If this is also the case for you, let's spend some time analyzing if we are totally powerless, or if we can do something to alleviate or at least mitigate our concerns.

When it comes to breaking out of the 9 to 5 work cycle and finding our own niche in a fulfilling career, we do have one primary advantage over the neurotypicals—our special interests. I've repeatedly seen instances where people on the spectrum have taken their childhood special interests and actualized these interests as adults into career opportunities. Gail Hawkins, an employment counselor (2004), who has helped many individuals with Asperger's find work, corroborates this observation. In the world of autism there are many well-known examples in which childhood special interests become meaningful adult work. One man with Asperger's had a fascination with maps since childhood. Today he works as a road commissioner and is very happy doing so.

Temple Grandin, a noted autistic, has become the ultimate expert on the humane treatment of animals. She has designed the facilities in which half the cattle are handled in the United States, consulting for firms such as Burger King, McDonald's, Swift and others. She has written bestselling books and taught or guest lectured at universities around the world. Her expertise grew from an early interest in the handling of livestock.

I have always had an interest in game shows, radio, and public speaking. My undergraduate degree was in communications, and I hoped to become a radio personality. Although I decided to take a different career path, I have had the opportunity to speak publicly, giving voice to subjects of interest. As a result of my current pursuits, I'm able to interject individuality into my work. Working at a company from 9 to 5 and taking orders from others all day has no appeal to me. It's important each of us aggressively seeks work that suits our individual needs, regardless of how skilled or unskilled the work.

Author Michael John Carley (2008) talks about what he believes are the two best work settings for people with Asperger's, one of which is the military. I believe that would be unendurable for me. Ironically, even though many people with Asperger's hate giving up their individuality, the armed forces appeals to many of us. According to Carley, the inherent structure of the military makes the work tolerable for some of us. Carley also recommends teaching at the college level, citing the relatively unstructured nature of higher education. This type of employment would be much more consistent with my individual needs. Teaching lacks the more rigid structure of the military and it allows an individual to retain more of a sense of self.

Carley lists the 9 to 5 business office as the most difficult setting in which to work for people with Asperger's. The competitive and fast-paced environment leaves people feeling like machines rather than human beings. The anxiety about answering in a certain way to your office boss for the next 40 years is a very normal and real concern for many people with Asperger syndrome.

Unconventional jobs seem to work for many of us on the spectrum. Have you ever heard of the "creative class"? Richard Florida (2003) defines the creative class as the group whose value is to create new ideas, new content, and new technology. The creative class is comprised of scientists, professors, writers, entertainers, artists, and engineers. Many of the men and women in these professions and job classifications highly value their individuality. They do not function like cogs in a machine. Rather, this group likes to invent, design, and build the machine itself. Does this sound like you? According to Florida (2003), the creative class makes up about 30 per cent of the American workforce, which is good news for people with Asperger's. I would venture the Asperger's population is well represented in the creative class.

However, to get to the place in which you can become a contributing member of the creative class and an autonomous, fully actualized human being, you need to deal with some of the *practical employment worries* associated with the workplace.

Practical employment worries

Unfortunately, the way the career ladder works is you start at the bottom. Granted there are exceptions. You often hear about high school graduates or college dropouts making a fortune on some new business venture. Perhaps the child of the successful businessperson has an inside edge to a quick rise in the business world. Most of us will not find ourselves in those circumstances. For most of us to join the creative class, we have to begin in the world of 9 to 5, starting at the bottom of the work chain and eventually moving ourselves up into a position that elevates us into the creative class. How can this objective be accomplished?

First, accept having to "pay your dues", putting the time in one position in order to gain the experience and knowledge that will lead you to the next position. Paying dues in a 9 to 5 job is probably going to take a heavier toll on you than on most neurotypicals. However, the payoff or reward is a possible entrée to the creative class in which you will be able to retain your individuality and your contributions will make a positive difference. To become a member of the creative class, you have to pay dues. In monetary and non-monetary terms, the dues are not cheap. You may have to go to college, learn your trade through vocational training, obtain a graduate degree and make some financial sacrifices.

But as you know, anything that is worth accomplishing is not going to come without some effort. In order to recap the ultimate benefit of doing what you want to do, for a while, you may temporarily have to take jobs you really don't want to do. How you frame these undesirable jobs is something to which you need to give serious thought. If you view a boring or monotonous job as a stepping stone to get you where you want to go (i.e. a means to an end), you may be able to maintain a sense of purpose, excitement, or anticipation about meeting your ultimate goal. If, however, you view a position as unacceptable, irrespective of where it might lead, then 9 to 5 work might not be worth it.

The practical worries come into play mostly vividly in the world of 9 to 5. Without a doubt, much of our anxiety on the job comes from others' expectations of our social behavior. While we don't appear to be handicapped, this hidden problem is our core deficit. In our discussion about cognitive-behavioral therapy, we talked about two ways to frame this real concern:

1. "I am a social misfit with no chance of ever succeeding in this company. People will see my defects even though I will pretend they don't exist."

or

2. "Working at this company will be a stepping stone for me. I will do whatever it takes to succeed here so I can ultimately have more job autonomy later on. If it means working harder to become more proficient in other areas important to the job, then I will do it."

As you can see, there is a dramatic difference in the perspectives of these two statements. The first one pre-supposes a life of misery, devoid of any joy. The other acknowledges the beginning of the journey will probably be a little rocky but eventually, things will get better. We all need hope in our lives. Without hope, life ceases to seem worthwhile. A person keeps hope alive by imagining a better future and by realizing the current situation will not last forever.

College as a sanctuary

College is considered something of a sanctuary for many individuals with Asperger's. College is less cruel than the competitive world of employment. In college, you are only responsible to yourself. In the workplace, you are responsible to your employer. In college, you pay tuition to be a student. In the workplace, people pay you to perform specific tasks or provide certain services. In college, you are still transitioning from the safe haven of living at home to the adult world of making a life for yourself. In the world of full-time employment, you are in the process of defining and sustaining your life.

In the senior year of college, a person with Asperger's sometimes comes to the realization the "real world" is right around the corner and the "real" anxiety sets in. Students can opt for graduate school, take some time off, or choose to enter the workplace. Ideally, if one chooses to enter the workplace after getting a bachelor's degree, he or she would have had sufficient internship experience to determine whether the career choice is a good fit.

Choosing a career haphazardly or by intuition alone can lead to a tremendous amount of anxiety once you begin working in your particular field. If you are a bit older and have already chosen a career that is currently making you miserable, there's no rule that says you have to stay locked in that career forever. In the 21st century, it seems people change their careers more frequently than what used to be the case. This does not mean you should find a new career every month or every year. You need to select a job in which you have the confidence to handle the work-related responsibilities in a field you passionately want to pursue.

Asperger's strengths

People with Asperger syndrome have tremendous strengths that should be highly valued by any prospective employer. Most of us with Asperger's are extremely honest, ambitious, innovative, and willing to go to great lengths to get the job done. To combat any anxiety associated with work-related issues that may arise, it's important to be confident regarding your strengths in any employment situation. Take time right now to think about some of your accomplishments. What qualities enabled you to perform so well? What environmental circumstances were in place to ensure you performed your work at the highest level possible? Make a list of those qualities and the circumstances that allowed you to do the best job possible. When you see this list in front of you, you will be able to recognize those environments that bring you into your element. Your dream job will not magically appear in front of you. You may also have to accept many jobs are not conducive to your needs. Instead of being miserable about accepting a less-than-ideal job, view the job as a way to get to a better opportunity. The important point is you have an end goal based on the special qualities you possess and the right environment to bring out those qualities.

Action points

- It is ideal to have an internship in a particular field to see if a field is right for you before committing to it.

- Most of us with Asperger's are extremely honest, driven, innovative, and willing to go to great lengths to get the job done. To combat any anxiety associated with work-related issues that may arise due to Asperger's, it's important to be confident regarding our strengths in any employment situation.

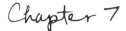

Selecting a psychotherapist

Ever since I was diagnosed with Asperger's (as an adult several years ago), I've been interested in how the mental health community responds to the needs of adults with autism spectrum conditions and, particularly, those with Asperger's. So far, I haven't been particularly impressed with the availability of quality services. In general, the focus of attention is primarily on young children and sometimes adolescents. Considering these young people grow up, I am disappointed the mental health community hasn't adequately responded by training qualified professionals to address the mental health needs of the adult Asperger's population. The task of finding a therapist who will be competent to match your unique psychological needs will admittedly not be an easy one, but it's possible. This chapter will provide you with some information to help you accomplish this objective, should you choose it.

First, I ask you to try to put aside whatever preconceived notions you have about psychotherapists. Some of you may believe a therapist is someone who should be able to solve all of your problems. Others may harbor a more hostile and distrustful attitude toward therapists. The fact is that therapists are human beings. As is true with any profession, some are learned and skilled, and some are lazy and incompetent, with many others in between. It is a particularly arduous task to find a good therapist because you can't discern a therapist's qualifications by simply looking at him or her. Looks can be deceptive. Therefore, I want to impart some information to assist you in finding the type of person who possesses the qualifications, skills, and credentials to meet your needs.

I feel qualified in addressing this issue for a number of reasons. First, I have been in a doctoral program in psychology for the past few years. My studies have afforded me the opportunity to interact with psychotherapists on a regular basis. From an academic standpoint, I have studied the necessary skills that contribute to being a good therapist as well as the different types of people that may need the services a good therapist provides.

Second, at various phases in my life over a number of years, I have been in and out of therapy, seeing more than a half dozen different therapists. Some of these therapists were life-saving. Others, in my opinion, should have chosen a different career path. I have seen and experienced the gamut, from the best to the worst, when in comes to mental health professionals. The last thing I would want you to do is pick a therapist haphazardly and run the risk of exposing yourself to psychological and emotional damage. Following the occasions I received bad professional guidance, I became invariably cynical of those who practiced psychotherapy. I went several years without seeing a therapist just because a therapist who *didn't* understand me wound up doing more damage than good. In those instances when I have been in therapy with a therapist who is understanding, encouraging, but also challenges me, the relationship is priceless. That kind of relationship can help you come to accept yourself as a valuable person on many levels—emotionally, mentally, and even spiritually. Most important to our discussion, a good therapist can help you to become less anxious.

Do you need psychotherapy?

That is a personal question. You may be in a position to benefit from it, but not be ready to undertake the challenge of the unknown. Perhaps the financial expense is a deterrent. Only you can determine whether your anxiety has become so problematic that it has interfered with your ability to experience joy and happiness on a regular basis. An anxiety disorder can often improve with insight, hard work, and even through certain prescribed medications, but sometimes, you need something more. There are times when even the strongest amongst us can't do it alone. The benefit of psychotherapy is being able to talk to someone who can specifically help address our unique emotional issues. A competent therapist can provide you with the individualized, real-time insight and feedback you can't acquire from any self-help book, including this one.

As we deal with the psychological issues people with Asperger's face daily, I hope you are becoming more aware of how these issues interfere with you developing your potential. We have been talking about some tools you can use to help overcome the obstacles in your life. A qualified therapist can tailor your sessions to work specifically on those areas of your emotional development that require improvement.

Does the therapist need to have expertise in Asperger's?

This is where it gets tricky. Most therapists won't have much expertise in treating autism spectrum disorders, including Asperger's among adults. Although due to the increasing demand for these types of services, academic programs are revising and updating training programs and curriculums. Seeing a therapist with expertise in Asperger's would be highly advantageous as far as finding someone who has the knowledge, skill, and training to understand your special needs and motives. However, this is not always realistic, particularly if you happen to live in a rural area. No matter where you live, you need to be extra selective and even downright skeptical about whether a particular therapist will be the right one for you.

If you decide to meet with a therapist, you have every right to ask him or her at the initial interview all the questions you want answered. Being inquisitive about a therapist's qualifications is not rude, it's intelligent, and any competent therapist will be comfortable with this type of interview. You would never dream of buying or leasing a car from a dealership without first asking all the questions you, as an informed consumer, wish to know. Similarly, before entering into what could be a long-term relationship with a significant investment of hope, time, and money, you need to be satisfied with the necessary information you have received from a given therapist. If you proceed with that therapist, you will continue to evaluate your experience based on your future encounters.

The first and most important question you'll want to ask is how knowledgeable is the therapist about Asperger's? Most likely, he or she will express some familiarity with the subject, but you need to know more. What specific experience—training and/or special coursework—has the therapist had in working with the Asperger's population?

Unless you're dealing with a highly qualified person in the field of autism spectrum disorders, you should inquire whether the therapist would be willing to learn more about the subject matter by doing some research, or perhaps even attending a seminar on Asperger's. If the therapist answers no to these questions or seems offended, thank this person politely as you immediately exit from the office. In my opinion, it is a major handicap for a therapist who doesn't have a basic understanding of the Asperger's experience to be effective in helping you control your anxiety. Consider this. If a therapist were trying to help a person from a culture different from his or her own, wouldn't it be prudent to learn about that culture? Wouldn't it also be logical to assume some of the problems the client is encountering may be stemming from cross-cultural expectations? The same is true with the Asperger's experience. It is unreasonable and even absurd to expect a therapist who possesses no clinical experience or working knowledge of Asperger's to be able to treat you effectively. If you have Asperger's, you have a different way of interpreting the world from sensory, emotional, and cultural viewpoints. How can we expect neurotypical therapists with no clue about Asperger's to understand our view of the world when there are such dramatic differences in perception? A good therapist will want to learn what it is like to be in our shoes. This is a reasonable expectation to have for any professional with whom you are considering to enter therapy.

Jim is an individual with Asperger's, in psychotherapy because of his issues with anxiety. His therapist, Dr. Crane, knows Jim has Asperger's but Dr. Crane has little clinical understanding of how to treat a person with Asperger's. During his weekly appointment, Jim explains he has a terrible time transitioning from the weekend to the workweek. Dr. Crane uses some CBT techniques to try to get Jim to understand Monday is just like any day of the week, but it's not effective in helping Jim reduce his anxiety. Next, Dr. Crane tries to get Jim to understand he's just had two days off so he should feel nice and refreshed. That doesn't work, either. Finally, Dr. Crane expresses his frustration toward Jim and says Jim is resisting treatment. Jim resents the accusation and decides to leave Dr. Crane's office, never to return.

Anyone who has basic knowledge concerning Asperger's would have been able to detect Dr. Crane's mistake in treating Jim. Crane overlooked the fact that making the transition from Sunday to Monday is extremely difficult for some individuals with Asperger's. They are just beginning to recover emotionally from the social demands of the past week of work. Without any empathy from Dr. Crane, or any understanding of the under-lying reason for Jim's anxiety, it is very unlikely Jim would be receptive to the cognitive reframing his therapist suggested. Dr. Crane may be effec-tive with his neurotypical clients, but he fails with Jim because of his lack of knowledge about Asperger's. I hope this scenario begins to shed some light on why it is so important to pick a therapist who understands and truly empathizes with the "Asperger's experience".

Eclecticism

While research seems to substantiate the effectiveness of CBT with our population, there are exceptions. A therapist with no clinical knowledge of Asperger's (like our Dr. Crane) may unwittingly try to help his client by trying to force him to see things differently, without realizing the person with Asperger's has issues unique to him. In trying to implement CBT without the therapist empathizing with the Asperger's experience, the result will most likely create a conflict between therapist and client. This is why it's important to try to evaluate a therapist's style at the outset. Ideally, a CBT practitioner should also be a good empathizer. Therefore, to meet all of your needs (knowledge of Asperger's and empathy), the therapist should be comfortable in utilizing different therapeutic modali-ties—CBT, psychodynamic, humanistic, etc.

Psychodynamic therapists tend to focus on your past history and psychological development. They make connections between early childhood memories (sometimes stemming all the way back to infancy) and your behaviors as an adult. They place a great deal of value on the unconscious mind. These therapists help you focus on your relationships with your parents, friends, lovers and others, and analyze how the relationships have affected you to this day. Another term for psychodynamic therapy is "insight therapy" because it can provide you with a great deal of insight about yourself. To some extent, schema-based therapy combines elements of psychodynamic therapy with CBT, with perhaps a stronger emphasis on the cognitive component.

Do I recommend this type of therapy? In the orthodox sense of lying on a couch for ten years talking about events from infancy and childhood, no, I do not. I do see its usefulness if it's incorporated as part of an overall treatment plan using other therapeutic modalities, such as the ones previously listed. I particularly recommend the use of this type of therapy if the emphasis is on helping you understand how certain early maladaptive schemas (EMS) may have formed.

We've already discussed humanistic therapists in an earlier chapter. The advantage of seeing a humanistic therapist is he or she will probably be the most interested and willing to learn about Asperger's than any other kind of therapist, since they pride themselves on being empathetic. However, because I highly value CBT and it empirically seems to work for those with Asperger's, I would still suggest finding someone who is eclectic but who also incorporates elements of humanistic psychology into his or her practice.

Psychoeducation

If you tell a therapist you want to receive some psychoeducation on social rules and norms (the hidden curriculum that most people know intuitively), I'm sure any diligent professional would be willing to accommodate you. In fact, any psychologist, counselor, or social worker with a basic knowledge of Asperger's would probably agree it would be time well spent between the two of you. Psychoeducation serves a dual purpose. While it is therapeutic in nature, it's also a teaching tool. There is an advantage to learning social rules and norms in a psychotherapist's office versus out in the real world. You can ask any question in the therapist's office without being judged negatively as dumb or ignorant. This is an environment where true learning can take place, where you can feel safe, respected, and cared for.

Sliding scales

Some therapists charge a fee based on a "sliding scale", meaning you pay based on your ability to pay, or your level of income. If you can find a good therapist who works on a sliding scale fee, by all means, take advantage of it. You should also make it a point to ask what types of insurance the therapist accepts and how the payment system works. Factoring finances into your decision to see a therapist is an important consideration. If you cannot afford to see a psychotherapist who doesn't have a sliding scale fee, perhaps there is a social worker or master's-level counselor at an agency who would be just as effective, yet much less expensive. In my opinion, many social workers and counselors can be just as effective therapeutically as the PhDs. The best way to find out about these people is to make inquiries. Similarly, colleges and universities may have clinics that offer mental health services to the public at a very low cost. The therapist may be a student in training, supervised by a professor.

Insurance

In psychotherapy, insurance companies will generally not cover the majority of your bill, as is more often the case if you were going to see an internist or primary care physician. In many cases with insurance, you will be obligated to pay about half of the total cost of the bill. Also, therapists will either be involved as participating providers with a managed care company or they won't be. If the therapist is a participating provider, it can mean to some degree, your confidentiality may be compromised, based on what the insurance company wants to know about you from your records. Insurance companies that are participating providers for therapists will sometimes limit the number of sessions covered under the policy, depending on the particular diagnosis or the terms of the coverage. Make sure you understand your coverage before embarking on a course of treatment with a therapist.

Whom should I ask?

Start by contacting your local Autism Society of America chapter. Ask them if they are familiar with any therapists in the area who work therapeutically with adults on the spectrum, particularly those with Asperger's. Just because you hear of someone who does work with our population does not automatically mean he or she is a good therapist or would be effective for you. It would be important to know if the therapist has a proven track record working with clients who have anxiety disorders.

Question a potential therapist in detail. Ask specific questions that will inform you:

1. How long have you been working with the Asperger's population?

2. What style (or modality) of therapy do you tend to find works best with our population?

3. Do you focus on long-term objectives or short-term treatment goals?

Ideally, you would want the therapist to be honest and tell you his therapeutic preference in terms of the style or modality he uses most frequently. You also want to know whether the therapist takes a highly individualistic approach with each client and doesn't use just one particularly modality with everyone who has Asperger's. Rather, he tailors the treatment approach to meet the specific needs of the individual. If a therapist with substantial clinical knowledge of Asperger's gives you the assurances to these types of considerations, chances are, you have found a good therapist.

Ask around your community. If you have a close relationship with your parents and they feel comfortable advocating for you, ask them to help you check out the names of competent and qualified therapists in the autism community. The therapist I see now is the result of some legwork on my part. I asked my parents to help me with my search and things worked out from there.

You can also visit this website therapists.psychologytoday.com/, which provides detailed listings for psychologists, psychiatrists, therapists, and counselors throughout the United States and Canada. Therapists often place their profiles on this website. In the profile, you usually find out how long the therapists have been practicing, where they went to school, what style of therapy they use, and what populations they specialize in serving, among other things. Remember, just because a therapist's profile looks appealing does not necessarily mean he or she will be a good fit for you. The therapist still needs to pass the "intangible test".

The intangible test

Assume you've just read about a therapist who, on paper, seems to fit all the qualifications you desire. He or she is an expert on Asperger's, practices eclecticism, and has a good track record as far as working with people who have anxiety issues. Does this automatically mean this therapist is someone with whom you should work? Not necessarily. I walked away from a therapist who had a renowned reputation working with adult clients with Asperger's. The problem was he started using an exclusive form of psychodynamic therapy that was ineffective in helping me. When I confronted him, he became irate and defensive claiming I was "questioning his professional abilities." Truthfully, from the beginning of my relationship with this therapist, something just did not feel right. I didn't trust my instincts. I let the fact that he was "an expert in adult Asperger's" override my own reaction about his ineffectiveness. Had I listened to my instincts, I would have saved myself a lot of time, money, and misery.

The best judge of whether a therapist is right for you is the "vibe" you pick up at the very first meeting. If it is an unpleasant vibe, do not continue to see this person. How will you know what kind of vibe you're picking up? You'll just know. If it feels pleasant to be with this person, if he or she is nice to chat with, seems to show some empathy on the first encounter, then he or she is probably a person with whom you can build a solid therapeutic relationship. These qualities are intangibles. You can't really put your finger on the precise qualities, but you just know when it feels right to you. Intangibles operate in real life all the time. From the moment you meet someone, sometimes you instantly know you are going to like that person. These same first impressions also apply to our judgment when seeking out a therapist.

Long-term therapy

There are certain qualities you should expect from your therapist if you are to continue the relationship over a period of time. The therapist should be able to handle any issue you bring up in therapy, no matter how dark or scary it appears on the surface. If you sense negativity or the therapist is being overly critical of you, you should feel comfortable mentioning this concern without the therapist becoming confrontational or defensive. Conflict and confrontations are inevitable, though, and even healthy in developing intimate relationships if you stay with a therapist for some time. It is the manner in which the therapist handles conflict that truly determines whether she is skilled at her profession. If the therapist becomes accusatory, angry or shows signs of counter-transference (when the therapist projects negative feelings onto you because you remind her of someone from the past), it is worth contemplating whether to end the relationship.

You also have the right to contact your therapist between sessions if emergencies arise. Of course, this privilege should not be abused. Any good therapist knows the issues you discuss during a session can often bring about extremely strong feelings between sessions.

Any competent therapist will also take threats of suicide seriously. If a therapist thinks you have a plan and are intent on following through with it, by law, he or she has to try to hospitalize you. Confidentiality applies to everything in therapy sessions except serious physical threats to one's self and others.

Action points

- Consider psychotherapy if your anxiety or depression has taken over your life. If you do not experience positive emotions on a regular basis, you may need some extra help.

- If you can't find a competent therapist in your area well versed in Asperger's, make sure the person would at least be willing to learn about Asperger's. Therapists without clinical knowledge of Asperger's might mistakenly apply treatments that won't work with you because they are treating you based on "neurotypical" standards.

- Psychoeducation is both a therapeutic tool and a teaching tool. If you feel you would benefit from it, request that your therapist employ the use of this technique with you.

- Investigate whether certain professionals in your area work with a sliding scale fee.

- Ask around in your local autism community to see if anyone knows of a therapist specializing in the ASD adult population. Just because one does, however, does not automatically mean he or she is an effective therapist. Trust your intuition when meeting the therapist to gauge whether this is a person you want to work with.

- Be watchful of how your therapist handles conflict, should it arise.

Chapter 8

Meltdowns

For some of the readers, I suspect this chapter may be the most pertinent to dealing with your anxiety. If there is one obvious way our anxiety outwardly manifests itself to the world, it is in the form of meltdowns (seemingly uncontrollable outbursts with no obvious antecedents). In this chapter, we are going to examine the role meltdowns play in our lives. Do they serve any useful purpose? If so, how can we harness their usefulness and use it to our advantage? On the flip side, what can we do to curtail meltdowns when they act as a destructive force in our lives and we lose control?

My experience with meltdowns

Ever since I can remember, meltdowns have been a part of my individual constitution. As a 31-year-old with Asperger syndrome, I have learned to control my meltdowns to a significant degree from when I was younger, but I can't honestly say I never experience them now. I'd be surprised if I ever eradicated meltdowns from my life. The difference is now I have an awareness and understanding about them and know when and where it is unacceptable to have a meltdown. I limit my meltdowns to the privacy of my condo as opposed to out in public.

My earliest memories of meltdowns are when I was about three or four. I remember hating to share the slide with other kids in the park. Being territorial, I assumed this was *my* slide. If other kids tried to use it after I slid down, but before I could get back on the ladder, I went ballistic. My parents viewed this with suspicion because they thought my behavior was inappropriate for my age.

Meltdowns usually occurred for me when something happened that didn't match the preordained script I had in my head for a given situation. These meltdowns could occur because of the most trivial reasons. Driving to Cleveland from Detroit with my parents at Thanksgiving was a thrill for me because they let me decide what route we would take. If there was any deviation from the route I selected, I would "lose it" emotionally. The mere thought of something not going according to my plan was terrifying for me. Because so many of our plans turn out to have unpredictable outcomes, my "first alert warning system" amygdala was always worried about something going wrong. I began anticipating the future with dread. Clinging to the predictable felt like trying to hold on to a handful of Jell-O on a warm day.

One night in high school, I had my first realization (an epiphany of sorts) that all of that these out-of-control episodes I had experienced over the years were meltdowns. From my limited perspective, I assumed everyone had these kinds of episodes regularly, so I didn't feel that guilty or troubled about having them. However, on this night I felt the wrath of judgment staring me in the face. We were celebrating Hanukah at my grandmother's house. As we were about to leave, my parents had to take care of some business somewhere and asked if my aunt and uncle would take me home. This shouldn't have been a big deal, but panic set in for me. I didn't want to go home with my aunt and uncle. Doing so meant I would have to socialize with them, something I was neither comfortable nor willing to do. I threw a huge fit in my grandmother's living room with the whole family witnessing this behavior. My parents were dumbfounded and undoubtedly embarrassed. Here I was, a high school student throwing a temper tantrum just because someone other than my parents would be driving me home. No one could understand how an otherwise mature high school student could act so infantile about something so trivial. In that moment, when all eyes of the family were focused on me during this meltdown, I realized my behavior was unusual.

Do meltdowns serve any legitimate purpose?

I have learned techniques for controlling meltdowns in public that I'm going to share with you. I'm even going to write about some strategies that may help you to control meltdowns while in the privacy of your own home. Does that mean I think meltdowns are something to be ashamed of? No, I don't. I look at meltdowns as being somewhat analogous to the physiological reaction of having to vomit. Vomiting is neither a good nor a bad thing. It's something that just happens and it usually serves a good purpose, which is to rid yourself of harmful contaminants in your stomach. But you would never want to vomit in public, would you? The first thing you would do when you began to get that nauseous feeling is head for the nearest sink or toilet to avoid any embarrassment or mess. It's not something you'd want to do in front of other people. Meltdowns are quite similar.

Do meltdowns serve any legitimate purpose? I believe they do, but only to a point. They release physical and mental tension, similar to the way having sex releases tension. If they are not protracted, they can help restore one's psychological equilibrium. Several years ago, I did a practicum at a school for autistic children and saw this principle in action. A physically large six-year-old boy was having a full-fledged meltdown. His teacher was gently restraining him so he wouldn't leave the room. During the restraining process, this boy was kicking, screaming, yelling and crying as hard and as loud as he could. After about ten minutes, his tantrum started to lose some of its force. After 15 minutes, this boy had exhausted himself to the point where he needed to rest. After resting for another ten minutes, he seemed to be fine and was participating in another activity. The meltdown seemed to have served a restorative function that 20 minutes later allowed him to feel emotionally balanced enough to participate freely in the next activity. If the meltdown serves any positive function for you, it should be cathartic. If you allow time to purge yourself of the tension and anxiety that has built up within you, as a result of dealing with many unpredictable things, it actually can make you feel restored and refreshed.

If I feel the need to have a meltdown, I'm conscious of that need and more in control over the manner in which I meet that need. I actually jump on my bed, hit a pillow against my wall and throw books down on the floor. In essence, I allow myself to have a little temper tantrum, and I don't feel guilty about having it. When I am done, I then force myself to relax and contemplate what I needed to purge from my system and learn from what happened. I've also worked on being much less attached to my mental "preordained scripts" than I used to be. I've tried to ignore the scripts altogether, since they frequently don't come to fruition. Why even set myself up for the disappointment and a possible meltdown in the first place?

Unpredictability

There are many things that happen throughout the day that make those of us with Asperger's susceptible to meltdowns: traffic jams, things not working (like cars and computers), getting sick, people not keeping promises, extra work, extra bills, long lines at the airport, delayed flights, unexpected telephone calls, last-minute requests from the boss, etc. As you can see, an array of unpredictable activities can take place.

As children, we consciously experienced our first unpredictable event. It could have happened when our parents made a promise they just weren't able to keep. After experiencing other unpredictable events occurring thereafter, our neurotypical counterparts began to see this phenomenon was a common event. Using Piagetian language, they assimilated the schema of unpredictability into their worldview from childhood and began to accept it as a part of life. Oddly, unpredictability became predictable. Whereas most neurotypicals learned this lesson from an early age, we did not. The unpredictability of the world is something most of us could never accept. How can a world that is supposed to operate in an orderly, Newtonian, and machine-like fashion be so darned unpredictable? If people say they are going to do things, then why don't they do them? If a flight is supposed to leave on time, why doesn't it? The fact is, our world is unpredictable, and it's about time we accept this truth.

Three of the four noble truths

The first noble truth of Buddhism is, "Life is suffering." Part of what I believe the Buddha was describing was the suffering we all experience, such as the process of being born (which can be traumatic), getting sick, maybe having marital difficulties and, eventually, dying. The Buddha was also wise enough to recognize the world is a place of impermanence and fluidity where things are always changing. In a changing world, we are bound to experience our share of turmoil and unpredictability. To resist this important truth would be like trying to paddle upstream in a canoe with the tide firmly pushing against you. The river is always going to be stronger than your arms will ever be.

The second noble truth states that the origin of suffering is attachment. The word attachment is not just referring to physical objects. We can also be attached to outcomes. Being attached to my preordained scripts left me miserable whenever they didn't materialize into reality. When I could loosen my attachment to outcomes, I found myself having fewer meltdowns. In other words, when I began to assimilate the concept of non-attachment into my mindset, I became less attached to outcomes and less anxious as a result. Hence, I have experienced fewer meltdowns.

The third noble truth states that even though life is full of suffering, we can choose an alternative path. The Buddha tells us transcending the suffering of this world is our birthright. In other words, we don't have to suffer. It's a choice. By letting go of the expectation that situations always go according to plan, we can alleviate much suffering and anxiety. It may seem counterintuitive for me to be asking you, as someone with Asperger's, to let go of your expectation that outcomes should go according to plan. In your life, you may feel like everything always seems to be spiraling out of control. As a result of this belief, you may try to control the few things you believe you can. Let me illustrate this point.

A few years ago, I attended a conference at Yale University. It wasn't a conference I was enjoying as much as I thought I would, and I couldn't wait to get on the plane and return home, get into my car, and drive home, where my music collection awaited me as well as a host of other things that enhanced my life. Because so many things during the course of this trip were beyond my control, I was greatly looking forward to being home, where I could resume total control of my surroundings. Upon boarding the airplane, the pilot proceeded to tell us the plane needed servicing and we were going to be delayed at least three hours. Then and there, I had a meltdown. People stopped and asked me if I was all right. One man even offered me a tranquilizer. It was *that* bad. I couldn't stop thinking the whole weekend was out of my control. Just when I thought I was finally going home to be back in control, something else went wrong.

Perhaps the world often feels out of control to you. To counter or at least neutralize the volatility you experience in our Darwinian jungle, you expect certain matters will go according to plan. This is our attempt to try and create order from an environment in which we experience chaos. Unfortunately, sometimes even our basic expectations end up deviating from what seemed like a sure thing. What if you could let go of your expectations and could view anything that happened as going according to plan? What if you always anticipated the possibly of chaos and accepted it when it resulted? If I had not held on so tightly to the idea of taking charge of my environment after the long weekend at Yale, I could have possibly avoided my meltdown on the plane. Just a small cognitive shift in perception and perspective can make the difference between having a meltdown and staying calm. Thus, it seems as if the Buddha was right: suffering can be alleviated, even though our lives are inherently filled with suffering. This is an interesting paradox to ponder in which opposite ideas seem reconcilable.

Transcending suffering

Did you ever hear of Norman Cousins? Mr. Cousins had a good reason to have a meltdown when, in 1964, soon after returning from a trip to Moscow, he learned he had contracted ankylosing spondylitis, a deadly collagen illness. Cousins (1979) started to experience excruciating symptoms of severe joint pain along with a fever. He exemplified what the Buddha described as true suffering. Here was Cousins, a middle-aged man facing death and experiencing agonizing pain. But that very suffering could not keep this man down. Instead, Cousins decided the best remedy to alleviate his dire circumstance was to laugh. He would spend hours every day watching Marx Brothers movies and found just by laughing, he was able to experience significant relief from his intense pain. The laughter served a function similar to the meltdown: a giant release. Tests later confirmed Cousins's laughter had lowered tissue inflammation. Since the publication of his book, *Anatomy of an Illness,* in 1974 describing the experience, "laughter therapy" has actually come into vogue. Medical science has proven laughter helps boost the immune system and promote health and healing. Cousins reportedly healed himself by remaining positive throughout his period of suffering through fits of laughter.

I tell you this story to illustrate how a person can choose not to suffer. Cousins exemplified the third noble truth—he transcended suffering. When we experience suffering in our daily lives because things do not always go according to plan, we should remind ourselves of Norman Cousins and laugh.

Creating order out of chaos

I believe the Asperger's experience can be summarized as follows: the attempt to create order out of chaos. Think of the great men and women who were thought to have Asperger's, and you'll find many of them had a burning desire to create order out of chaos: Albert Einstein, Sir Isaac Newton, Alan Turing, and the list goes on. Even if a person with Asperger's is not scientifically oriented, I still believe the driving force in the life of an individual with Asperger's is to create order out of chaos. Those of us with a strong desire to bring about social justice amid social chaos might choose to become lawyers. Others write computer software programs, creating technological efficiency where there was once chaos. People with Asperger's who create beautiful music are creating harmonies out of otherwise chaotic sounds.

The source of meltdowns occurs when attempts to create order out of chaos fail. Think about the times in your life when you experienced a meltdown. These incidents almost always occurred when you anticipated and were fearful of the oncoming chaos. But is chaos always a bad thing? If you could alter your perspective about chaos and even come to understand or appreciate it, it would be possible to establish a new relationship with things not going according to plan.

Chaos theory (Blitz, Carlson and Carlson 1998) states that while it may look like there is an apparent lack of order in the universe because of the chaos we see on the surface, there actually is an order to everything we observe. This theory has been used to predict the stock market, the weather, and pretty much anything else in the process of unfolding. Chaos maintains the order of the universe. By coming to embrace rather than fear chaos, we can begin to understand how our concept of order was fueling our meltdowns. The chaotic circumstances of your life have led you to the exact place you find yourself today. If you were to look back and examine all the events in your life, you would see they unfolded quite methodically. At the time you experienced these chaotic events, they seemed anything but methodical. However, now that some time has passed, you can begin to understand why those events occurred. Perhaps you met someone who introduced you to someone else who helped you land your first job, where you then met your wife, etc. Or perhaps something bad occurred such as a major death in the family or the loss of your best friend and those events taught you the values of having inner strength and a sense of independence. You would never have experienced these things without first enduring the aforementioned hardships.

When we experience a meltdown, we are in the midst of chaos. It helps to maintain the awareness that perhaps the situation is actually a test of our mental and emotional fortitude. By taking on the attributes of the Buddha and Norman Cousins, we rise above the suffering and chaos that is so inherent in life and in the process of doing so, increase the opportunity for meaning and purpose in our lives through the establishment of order. Perhaps order results by enduring chaos and reflecting upon it afterwards.

Yet again, we confront an interesting paradox. By embracing chaos instead of resisting it, we can paradoxically create order. When a meltdown occurs, it is serving up a moment to learn. Ask yourself what you need to discover to grow from the circumstance that is upsetting you or causing you to be anxious. Use the meltdown as an opportunity to grow as well as let off some steam.

Uncertainty

I believe the biggest challenge for any individual with Asperger's is to embrace uncertainty because it also means accepting chaos. Susan Jeffers (2003) author of *Embracing Uncertainty* believes the key to a life of peace and serenity is to let go of expectations. She compares life to that of watching a movie. We get very annoyed with people who tell us how a movie ends before we have even had a chance to see it because we enjoy experiencing the movie ourselves. For most of us, watching a movie in which we know what will happen would be boring. Jeffers wonders why we can't take that same approach with our own lives. If you knew you were going to get cancer at the age of 45 or 65, would the knowledge spur you to maximize your enjoyment of life? Would you want to know if you knew you were going to win the lottery in 20 years? You may think so at first, but the knowledge would probably interfere with your life until you hit the jackpot. You would likely sacrifice living your life in the present moment.

By anticipating future events, you are creating the circumstances for future meltdowns. For example, if you believed for years you were going to win the lottery and on the day you bought your ticket, you didn't win, you would be incredibly disappointed, maybe even devastated to the point of a meltdown or worse. However, if you bought a lottery ticket without the preconception of winning and didn't win, you wouldn't feel nearly as disappointed because chances are you weren't expecting to win. By remaining attached to the outcome of future events, you are ensuring a meltdown will take place when those future events don't come to fruition. Detaching yourself from the outcome, on the other hand, helps you to enjoy the present moment more fully. Staying detached also helps you see the larger picture with more clarity and without becoming too bogged down in the details.

Action points

- Use meltdowns to serve a cathartic function for you.
- You can transcend suffering by lessening your attachments to various outcomes, thus lessening anxiety and preventing meltdowns.

Chapter 9

Anxiety and shame

At first glance, it might not seem obvious how the emotions of shame and anxiety are related to one another, but if you've been reading this book closely, you have probably figured it out. We've talked about how, if we are not careful, our early shameful and maladaptive schemas can induce fear by forcing us to distort situations cognitively. In this chapter, I'll discuss how shame and anxiety are closely intertwined, as an understanding of this connection will help to facilitate emotional healing for you.

Asperger's and shame

In the chapters on Asperger's and anxiety, CBT and mindfulness, the salient point was how schemas and core beliefs (can) make you feel shameful about yourself and why they potentially make you more anxious and less clearheaded about life. The information from these chapters is vital in terms of now exploring the precise mechanisms with which shame operates. Shame usually is a precursor to anxiety, not the other way around. When you begin to feel shameful about yourself, a host of defense mechanisms begin to activate to guard you against that shame. One of the purposes of these defense mechanisms is also to make you less anxious about your perceived personal deficiencies. We talked earlier about one of those defense mechanisms, overcompensation. There are others, but for purpose of our discussion, it's important to remember shame is usually at the root of these defenses.

Having Asperger's means you were often misunderstood as a child and possibly as an adult, too. Teachers most likely couldn't understand why you had such inconsistencies between your academic and social intelligence and probably scolded you on more than one occasion to "just try harder". Perhaps your parents grew frustrated and impatient with your frequent meltdowns. Peers taunted, teased, and bullied you throughout much of your schooling. It's important to understand living through such constant criticism and disapproval can definitely scar one's psyche. According to recovery expert John Bradshaw (1988), we store these traumatic, shame-based incidents within our memory. We lock these memories in time and never truly forget them. They exist in our unconscious, forever exerting their influence on how we view ourselves and others, until we consciously recognize the memories for what they are—outdated relics from the past.

Let's look at how experiencing certain shame-inducing situations repeatedly can lead to increased anxiety later in life:

1. James was constantly belittled and humiliated for his handwriting and art skills. In college, he freezes up whenever he has to write a term paper, even if he's using a computer.

2. Classmates repeatedly told Rajiv he was weird and a freak. Years later, Rajiv tries extra hard to be an ultra-conformist, ashamed of who he is and terrified others will see through his efforts.

3. Jennifer's peers tormented her for being a tomboy. Years later, she tries to hide her sexuality because of the memories associated with the bullying she received.

4. Peers in elementary school teased Pete relentlessly for liking classical music. Now, as an adult, he will only listen to it privately.

Disavowing parts of the self from the whole self

Did you notice the pattern that emerged for these individuals? Motivated by fear, they each disowned the part of themselves that they were ashamed of. Bradshaw (1988) calls this "the creation of the false self". This "false self" is very similar to the existential psychologists' concept of the false self. I call it disavowing certain parts of yourself from your whole self. You're trying to cover up and dispose of those parts of yourself that you're ashamed of. A trauma or series of events was so strong that you sent those parts of yourself into hiding. You've conditioned yourself to believe you are flawed based on these early experiences. You believe if you can disavow yourself from the shameful parts of your personality, you'll be a better person. The more this fallacy remains a part of your thinking, the greater the amount of anxiety you will experience. This fallacy, ironically, also leads to perpetual shame.

Let's consider the examples in greater detail: James disavowed his potential creative spark for writing because of the belittling comments his teachers made. His future fear, based on his past trauma, is he doesn't want to be viewed as a failure due to his poor writing skills. Rajiv disavowed himself from his individuality and creativity because of being labeled a freak by his classmates. His future fear is to be viewed as an outcast. Jennifer disavowed herself from her true sexual orientation because of strong negative memories of being viewed as a tomboy by her classmates (this is not to say all tomboys receive negative feedback or are lesbians). Her future fear is she does not want to experience lifelong discrimination at the hands of society. Pete has disavowed himself from an interest in classical music because his peers viewed him negatively for having certain musical tastes. Pete's future fear is he will never be able to express his individuality.

How do I see this behavior manifested in adults with Asperger's? I have met some adults with a diagnosis of Asperger's who don't want to talk about their Asperger's at all. It's not a part of their vernacular. I strongly suspect the stigma of having Asperger's and what it represents in their minds is just too painful to deal with. When they think of the word "Asperger's", perhaps they become fearful having Asperger's will undermine their next job interview, date, or social encounter because that's what has happened so many times in the past. To disavow oneself from Asperger's is to try to appear as neurotypical as possible. Thus, the person lives in denial of a part of his or her reality. Perhaps when they think of the word Asperger's, they're reminded of all the negative and traumatic experiences from their youth, and to distance themselves from those memories, they effectively distance themselves from the concept of having Asperger's. In doing so, what emotional price do they pay? I'll tell you: They are suppressing parts of their unique and wonderful personalities to try to fit in more with others. They are also missing the opportunity to meet other individuals with Asperger's, a possible source of strength and support. They have decided having Asperger's is what makes them flawed human beings, and if the Asperger's were somehow to go away, their lives would improve.

Shame and depression

To disavow and renounce certain aspects of yourself isn't a healthy undertaking, but it's better than disavowing the whole self. According to Bradshaw (1988), when you disavow your whole self, you take on the identity of a complete and utter failure. In your mind, everything about you screams failure. Since the whole self seems unacceptable, you can't even cast off a part of yourself. With enough exposure to trauma and repeated reinforcement from the external world, a person can conclude he or she is an entirely defective human being. For many, the only solution to this problem is to commit suicide. By the time a person reaches this state of mind, he or she feels numb to the core. While anxiety, shame, and dysthymia might have been contributing factors to the first stage of disavowing aspects of the self from the whole self, this more serious stage is usually represented by an onset of major depression. If you are feeling suicidal, I urge you to contact a mental health professional immediately or at least tell someone how you feel.

You have to confront consciously how you first came to believe in your total worthlessness. As you search for the primary cause, you'll eventually come to understand you had intrinsic value all along and still do. Your whole self isn't a failure, and you are and always were a person of significant self-worth. Society is just not always fair and tolerant when it comes to those who are different. If you have accepted the belief you are a complete failure, it is likely the result of your having adopted the negative reactions you received from certain people. It is likely that other people's reactions were related to the differences they perceived, differences relating to Asperger's, over which you lacked control.

Perhaps you think of yourself as a failure because of job struggles. Perhaps it's because you have trouble staying in a romantic relationship. Perhaps socializing feels like an onerous task because the necessary skills do not come naturally. Maybe it's some or all of the above. Whatever the reason, think of Albert Einstein who, as a child, was constantly told how slow and stupid he was. Think of Michael Jordan who didn't make his high school varsity basketball team. Think of news anchor Katie Couric who was told early in her career she entered the wrong profession because she had no talent. Think of me. I was diagnosed with a learning disability in written expression for most of my years in public school, and now I'm working on my second book. All of us could have easily viewed ourselves as partial or complete failures, but we didn't. You don't have to, either. I guarantee there is a place for you in this world, regardless of your past success or failures. We all have gifts and talents. The purpose of life is to awaken them.

If feeling like a failure is so ingrained in you that CBT fails to convince you otherwise, you might try reliving some of these traumatic scenes through techniques like eye movement desensitization and reprocessing (EMDR) and/or hypnosis. It's also important to remember biological factors often work in tandem with psychological ones, which is why most treatment professionals recommend a combination of psychotherapy and medication for the treatment of depression.

Shadow dancing

Whether or not you would like to admit it, you have a dark side. We all do. Carl Jung, the founder of analytical psychology, called this dark side "the shadow" (Edinger 1972). Part of what the shadow represents are the parts you think you have already disavowed from yourself. The only problem with thinking you have disavowed these parts of yourself is they don't automatically disappear. Unfortunately, what you think you have disavowed ultimately remains stored, even if it's in the unconscious.

The shadow contains both positive and negative aspects. The positive elements are the qualities you tried to disavow from yourself because of societal and/or environmental pressures. The negative elements are the basic, animalistic drives within you that are scary to acknowledge—what

Sigmund Freud (Kahn 2002) called the *id*. We call the shadow the dark side of who we are because it acts inconspicuously and tries not to be noticed. Yet, the paradox is that the more the shadow goes unnoticed, the more power and influence it has on our behavior. The more it goes unnoticed, the more shameful we feel and the more anxious we become.

The shadow can cause you a great deal of undue stress and misery if you do not know how it operates in your life. By staying hidden, the shadow convinces you it does not exist. If you became aware of its existence, you would recognize it as part of your humanity, and its danger would recede. The shadow tries to get you to believe as long as you deny a part of yourself, no one else will ever think a bad thought or harbor an unhealthy or even destructive thought toward you. It wants you to think you are unique in this sense. By feeling unique, you become more anxious and depressed. In this case, you are not unique. The shadow is a universal archetype, which means it exists within everyone.

Lee Baer (2002) who is an expert on obsessive-compulsive disorder says the more a person tries to repress specific thoughts or urges, the stronger those thoughts and urges will persist in one's consciousness. A simple example will demonstrate this observation: right now, I'd like you *not* to think about cows for 30 seconds. Do your very best to think of anything but cows... Well, what's the first thing that happened? You thought of a cow, of course, simply by trying not to think of a cow. It's like instructing a child not to think about candy.

The shadow works the same way. When you don't recognize you have a shadow and unknowingly repress it, you begin to try to divorce yourself from all the "bad" aspects of who you really are, not realizing by doing so, those parts of you are going to try that much harder to find self-expression in another way. By trying to disavow yourself of these characteristics, you build up tension within your psyche because what you disavow usually rebels against you and will always be seeking a way to be heard, regardless of whether you want it to or not. Trying to suppress or unconsciously repressing your shadow is the same as trying not to think of the cow. The picture of the cow only grows stronger in your mind by trying not to think about it. Similarly, the shadow grows in strength by suppressing or repressing it, consciously or unconsciously.

Integrating negative shadow aspects

Dealing with the negative side of the shadow is never easy because it's the scariest part of who we are as human beings. By confronting the shadow, you are dealing with the part of you that scares you the most. It's no wonder many people won't admit its existence. That's the irony of the shadow; the scarier the shadow is, the more you'll want to deny its presence and the more power it will gain over you.

According to Baer (2002), many normal people have urges to do some of the most heinous acts imaginable. He tells of a mother who was constantly paralyzed by the fear of harming her infant child; a young man who was afraid of striking innocent bystanders in a crowd, and a driver visualizing himself steering his car into a pedestrian. They all had a genuine fear that a switch could be flipped and they would act out these gruesome fantasies. They worried obsessively. Baer (2002) says millions of people have such disturbing fantasies, thoughts, or urges, suggesting they are not as uncommon as most of us would like to believe. By trying to suppress these negative shadow aspects of your personality, you create more of an urge to commit these unspeakable acts. Paradoxically, by accepting these feelings as part of what it means to be human, you take away the power these feelings have over you because they are seen for what they are—normal and basic human/animalistic instincts. By accepting these feelings and urges, it is more likely you will never act on them. You have conscious control over them.

The best way to deal with negative shadow aspects is to accept these feelings and urges for what they are and then sublimate them, as we talked about earlier. Judging these feelings sends them underground, where they will have more power over you. Accepting those feelings means you can consciously fuel them into more constructive pursuits. If, for example, you feel the need to hurt someone physically, forgive yourself for having that urge, then buy a punching bag. You'll get some exercise as a bonus. If you feel the need for revenge, forgive yourself for feeling that way, then beat someone in a game of Scrabble, or some other competitive endeavor in which you feel confident of the outcome. The way I dealt with anger toward bullies when I was a schoolboy was to funnel my energy into winning a tennis match. Instead of trying to lash back at the bullies—which I was tempted to do—I redirected my anger in a healthier and more socially acceptable way, beating opponents on the tennis court.

The two key factors in this equation are:

1. Forgiving yourself.

2. Sublimation.

When you can free up the energy you use to keep the negative part of your shadow hidden, you ensure its destructive forces do not wreak havoc in your life. By accepting these urges for what they are, you can channel these desires toward more constructive pursuits. You can't do this as long as the urges remain hidden from view. As long as the urges remain underground, it is more likely one day, the metaphoric switch will flip, and there will be unintended consequences.

Integrating positive shadow aspects

What makes certain comedians so funny? A lot of them have taken their constructive anger and quirky personalities and fused those qualities into hilarity. Many great comedians talk about the fact that a substantial portion of their routine involves channeling a dark or angry side of their personalities onstage. You can see this in the work of the late George Carlin or the late Andy Kaufman. Similarly, some great writers are known for producing beautifully poignant, sometimes sad and tragic pieces of work that highlight certain shadow aspects of themselves. Their writings artistically reflect the true depths of their souls.

What positive shadow aspects do you need to reclaim? Only you can answer that question. But as someone who knows the Asperger's population fairly well, I can say many people with Asperger's are ashamed of their quirkiness. They see it as a bad thing. They try not to appear eccentric and as a result, end up being more socially clumsy and anxious than they would be if they accepted their traits. Denying one's quirkiness doesn't make the quirkiness go away, but accepting one's quirkiness and even embracing it as a part of the real self can afford a creative outlet that was previously blocked.

The more you deny who you are, the more you bury your true personality. By accepting yourself, you alleviate a tremendous amount of anxiety and free up those aspects of yourself currently dormant.

Action points

- Be aware that trauma-based shame plays a great role in repressing parts of your personality you deem to be shameful.

- Bear in mind that the more unaware you are of your shadow, the more anxious and shameful you will be. As the Oracle of Delphi proclaims, the path to wholeness is to know who you are, warts and all!

- To integrate negative shadow aspects, you need to accept those urges, drives, and fantasies as a part of being human, and forgive yourself for having them. Then, you need to sublimate these drives into more constructive activities.

- To integrate positive shadow aspects, you need to reclaim the parts of yourself you once disavowed. Accept yourself for who you are.

Chapter 10

Anxiety and health

Throughout most of the book, we've been exploring anxiety from primarily psychological and cognitive points of view. In this chapter, we're going to examine the mind-body connection.

My story

For many years, I took very poor care of myself physically. My drug of choice was food. Every time I felt overwhelmed, I reached for food or ordered double portions from restaurants. Feeling satiated left me temporarily less anxious and even gave me a bit of a high. Yet within 20 minutes or so, those feelings would fade, and I would feel more depressed and anxious than before. This pattern of binge eating lasted for almost a decade. From time to time, it's still something I continue to struggle with, though I have made some improvements. Ironically, as a result of my poor food choices over the years, I have become more anxious about my health than I would have been, had I dealt with my anxiety more effectively in the first place.

Two years ago, I received some upsetting news from my internist. I was diagnosed with Type II diabetes. That wasn't all. Based on the results of preliminary tests I had undertaken, I was also going to need angioplasty. I was shocked. How could a 29-year-old who used to be in perfect health suddenly be a candidate for a procedure most people don't need until they are over the age of 50? There was a logical explanation, and it was painfully obvious. I came to the realization because of the ineffective ways that I had been dealing with my anxiety, I had unwittingly created for myself an even bigger fear—death. One of the reasons why I wrote this book is because I understand from my own personal experiences the devastating consequences that can arise from dealing with anxiety ineffectively. I want to caution others not to make the same mistakes I have.

A few weeks after the visit to the internist, I got a call from my cardiologist. He wanted to run one more series of tests to rule out any false positives. As I waited for the results, I contemplated what it would be like to have a catheter enter my body while I was under sedation. It was a chilling thought. I wondered if I was dying and had a full-fledged panic attack.

The next day, I found out the initial tests were false positives, and I wasn't going to need angioplasty. While the pent-up anxiety evaporated, I now knew I had acquired a chronic disease, and it was most likely the result of my bad choices. In that moment, I realized my diabetes was something I probably could have prevented, had I been able to deal with my anxiety more effectively. It was in that exact moment the idea for this book was born. I knew I could help myself by helping others learn from my mistakes.

How am I doing now? I have my good days and my bad days. But I'm fully aware when I let my anxiety get the better of me and use food as my drug of choice, I am probably shortening my lifespan with each bite of unhealthy, carbohydrate-filled food I eat. Keeping that thought in my mind has helped me go forward whenever I need to be reminded about the risks of complacency.

Routines and exercise

I learned something very important about my dad several years ago. He was significantly out of shape when my mother was pregnant with me. He was a heavy smoker, ate unhealthy foods, and didn't pay much attention to his physical well-being. Realizing he was soon going to be a father, he became scared he might not be around to see me grow up unless he made some significant changes. In 1977, the year I was born, he made a commitment—at the age of 34—to quit smoking, change his diet, and run eight miles a day, never before having been a serious athlete of any kind. He quit smoking, eliminated red meat from his diet and has continued his running routine for the past 30 years (cutting down to four miles a day in the last few years) and only taking days off in extremely inclement weather or when he's ill. When I ask my dad if he enjoys running, he told me running is like a drug for him. If he is not able to run in the morning, he feels lousy all day long. He serves as an inspiration to me to illustrate how people can change their behavior in positive ways.

In listening to my dad, I couldn't help but think of people with Asperger's. Like my father, we, too, seem to be creatures of habit. Our routines are like holy rituals. We wouldn't skip them or miss them for the world. Making exercise a part of your daily routine is not only essential for flexible joints, a strong heart, and longevity, it also helps to reduce psychological anxiety. Speaking from my own experience, nothing melts away tension like playing a good game of tennis, swimming laps in a pool, or briskly walking my dog. Your body produces endorphins whenever you exercise. From a physiological point of view, this creates a similar feeling to being high on a drug. Your body learns to crave this feeling. If it doesn't get it, it starts to atrophy. No one wants to have an old body while they are still young.

In addition to taking care of your body physically, it is just as important to take care of your body mentally.

Mind-body connection

Science has fully accepted an ancient piece of wisdom: the mind influences the body. Dr. Deepak Chopra (1987), a metaphysical teacher and pre-eminent mind-body expert, explains disease often shows up in the body as a result of anxiety and stress. According to Dr. Chopra, hypertension, ulcers, headaches, insomnia, backaches, shortness of breath, and a host of other ailments can be traced back to poor stress management. Chopra acknowledges that addictions (like my eating addiction) and obsessive thoughts and behaviors can also occur because of poor stress management.

In recent years, there has even been evidence to suggest parts of the body, other than the brain, register emotions the same way the brain does. Dr. Paul Pearsall (1999), a respected psycho-neuroimmunologist, suggested the heart also thinks and feels like the brain. This seems like a radical notion, but he showed many of the same neural cells that are found in the brain are also found in the heart. In her 1997 book, *A Change of Heart*, Claire Sylvia described what happened to her after her heart transplant. According to Sylvia (1997), after she received her new heart, she experienced a major change in her personality. Further, new memories and sensations surfaced from out of nowhere. She ultimately sought out the family of the young man who had donated his heart. To her utter surprise, she found out she had seemingly acquired some of his personality traits. Even more surprising, her story is not unique. Apparently, reports of this phenomenon of a personality transfer are not uncommon among heart transplant recipients (Pearsall 1999).

Several authors in recent years have taken this discovery to new heights by writing about it in the self-help genre for general readers. Two of those authors are Doc Lew Childre and Howard Martin, founders of the HeartMath Solution Program. Childre and Martin (1999) believe the heart is not just a pump, but that it has an intelligence of which most people have been previously unaware. They explain the brain and the heart are meant to stay in sync with one another but often don't, due to emotions such as anxiety, depression, and anger, which create a state of incoherence and disarray in both organs. According to the concept of entrainment, when two pendulum clocks are beside one another, eventually they should come to swing in synchrony (Childre and Martin 1999). The concept is exemplified among women who live together for a long period of time and start having concurrent menstrual cycles (Washington 1996), or when a married couple (who looked nothing alike when they got married) start resembling each other physically and displaying similar mannerisms. In the same way, the natural state of the brain and the heart is to be in an entrained state. To get the brain and heart entrained, Childre and Martin offer us the "freeze frame" technique.

Imagine you are watching a sporting event. Why is there the need for instant replay? Because you can see what happened in clearer detail when you are observing the action in slow motion rather than in real time. The freeze-frame principle operates on the same premise. When you can slow down your mind, you can see things with greater clarity. Sounds a bit like CBT, but the main difference is Childre and Martin suggest you accomplish this task with your heart, not your brain. To paraphrase their five-step freeze-frame process:

1. Be aware of when you feel anxious or stressed and freeze that emotion.

2. Turn off the thoughts of your mind and focus on what your heart seems to be telling you for at least ten seconds.

3. Recall a fun, peaceful, or calm experience, episode, or feeling in your life. It could be when you were listening to your favorite music, or when you won an award, or even wrote new codes for computer software.

4. After recalling this episode, ask your heart what would be a better response to the stress than the one you used.

5. Listen to what your heart says. In my own experience, the answer is found often in silence, not through mental pictures or words.

By tuning into a positive memory, you neutralize any negative and unproductive reaction from your reactive amygdala. These positive feelings (from a health point of view) also provide regeneration to the immune and hormonal systems (Childre and Martin 1999). By slowing down and listening to the intelligence of the heart, one can improve his or her physical health and in the process and gain newfound clarity from previously distressing issues. Childre and Martin have taught tens of thousands of people how to use these techniques successfully. If we acknowledge the heart is not just a pump but also an intelligent, living, breathing organ, we might benefit from its wisdom. If the heart and brain are entrained and not at odds with each other, it would make sense our health would naturally improve as a consequence of these organs working in harmony.

In addition to the heart, the rest of the body also seems to think and feel as well. Candice Pert (1997), internationally recognized, coined the term "neuropeptide," which is a chemical messenger that travels throughout the body, mirroring our emotions. According to Pert, these chemical messengers actually respond to our emotions and can be found in other parts of the body beside the brain, including various organs, tissue, skin, muscles, and the endocrine glands. What this means is the entire body is capable of storing emotional memories. For example, it is possible that if you experienced trauma in a certain part of the body, that body part will remain traumatized until those frozen memories are released.

As a child, my teachers often yelled at me. The most frequent was my art teacher. She ridiculed my bad penmanship and poor artistic performance in front of the class. These memories are still so vivid that to this day, whenever I pick up a pencil and write something, my hand shakes, almost as if it is reliving the trauma of this teacher humiliating me.

The real value of knowing about the mind-body connection relates back to one of the major themes of this book. As we've discussed in the chapters on CBT and mindfulness, maladaptive thoughts lead to more anxiety and poor mental health. As we have seen in this chapter, negative thoughts and emotions also lead to poor physical health. If the body is as responsive to our thoughts and emotions as science seems to suggest, it's safe to assume maladaptive thoughts aren't just bad for the mind, they are bad for the entire body.

Anti-anxiety medication

According to Luke Tsai (2001), professor of psychiatry and pediatrics at the University of Michigan, psychotherapeutic medications can sometimes be helpful in alleviating the symptoms of anxiety for people with Asperger syndrome and autism. I do not consider myself an expert on these medications, but I can tell you there are several different drug classes that treat anxiety disorders including anti-convulsants, beta blockers, monoamine oxidase inhibitors, and serotonin reuptake inhibitors. Some of the drugs increase the function of GABA, (gamma amino butyric acid), an inhibitory neurotransmitter sometimes deficient in ASD individuals. Some drug classes enhance serotonin production and others inhibit adrenaline production. The important point to remember is these pills are not a panacea. They are meant to help take the edge off and make it easier for you to manage your anxiety. Temple Grandin has spoken publicly about how certain psychotherapeutic medications have been life-saving for her. I heard an interview she gave on National Public Radio in which she said without her medication, she would be an entirely different person. Medication works, but you must do a large portion of the work as well.

My own experience in taking anti-depressants and anti-anxiety medications has shown me drugs do help me reach an equilibrium. I would have found it too difficult to engage in the work of CBT and mindfulness without these daily medications. The decision to start taking these medications is a serious one. It isn't something you should do on a whim. You need to understand the possible side effects associated with each drug, the withdrawal effects, and assess how you might further your personal goals along with taking the medications. If you believe these drugs will work wonders for you, I'm here to assure you that won't happen. Just like anything in life that is worthwhile, alleviating anxiety takes hard work; a pill alone won't do it.

A caveat: make sure the psychiatrist or internist who prescribes your medication has some familiarity with ASD. A basic knowledge of autism and Asperger's would most likely inform the clinician as to subtle differences in dosaging and even the type of medication he or she would prescribe to you. At the very least, the doctor needs to have worked with children who have autism or Asperger's but, preferably, adults too. If you decide to try medication as part of the process for reducing your anxiety, do see a therapist at the same time.

Action points

- Take good physical care of yourself. The better your health is, the less you'll have to worry about in life. No one is in total control of his or her health, but our conscious acts can play a role in determining health or disease. Don't leave your health to chance.

- Make exercise a part of your daily routine. You'll find it reduces anxiety, makes you feel good, and improves your overall physical health.

- If you're not careful about how you manage stress, your mind has the power to create a host of physical ailments. Keep this in the forefront of your mind!

- Certain anti-anxiety medications can be helpful, but they are not panaceas. Find a doctor who has some knowledge of ASD and Asperger's to prescribe your medication.

Chapter 11

Anxiety and spirituality

I grew up in an agnostic household. The topic of God or religion was seldom, if ever, mentioned. It wasn't until I became a freethinking adult that I started to question some of the assumptions I had grown up with as a child. Most of those assumptions revolved around the notion that all that exists is what can be observed on a material plane (e.g. what is seen, heard, felt, tasted or smelled). As I started to become more inquisitive, I talked to many different people and read a lot of spiritually oriented material. The conclusions I have come to, based on a preponderance of the evidence, suggest to me there is more to life than meets the eye.

How is this relevant to the discussion of anxiety? Before I respond, I'd like to answer another question you may have right now. I want to say emphatically that I do not intend to sway you to a particular religion in this chapter. All of the opinions expressed within this chapter are mine and mine alone. This chapter is not as scientifically rigorous as the rest of the book has been up until now. While the rest of the book has been substantiated by research and empirical evidence, this chapter represents my personal viewpoints. Nothing more, nothing less.

Though I was born Jewish, I do not subscribe to the teachings of any specific religion. Rather, I believe all religions have something valuable to teach us. The point of this chapter will be to survey what some of the great spiritual traditions have to say about stress management. Even if you don't happen to believe in God, you might find something valuable within this chapter.

I strongly believe all life is interconnected. This spiritual realization has actually helped me to become less anxious because I don't feel like an island unto myself. I see how we are all in this together. My own personal worries pale in comparison to the larger concerns about Planet Earth.

There are two basic ways to view oneself in relationship to the world. One is to see yourself as totally isolated and separate from everything else, in which case all of your worries are unequivocally yours. Seeing yourself as separate from the rest of the world locks you into a prison where your problems intensify because there is no breathing room for them. On the other hand, seeing yourself as interconnected to the world not only puts your worries into perspective, but also puts life into perspective. What this dramatic principle of interconnectivity means is you are never really alone. You are a mighty being possessing more power than you are probably aware of. Just as a butterfly flapping its wings in Kansas has the potential to cause a cyclone in Japan (according to chaos theory), you, too, can cause extraordinary things to happen. And let's face it, you have a lot more potential than a butterfly. If you can own the power you have, you'll trust yourself more. In trusting yourself, you'll become less ambivalent about who you are and your role in the world. You'll eventually become more comfortable with embracing whatever life throws at you and dealing with the eventuality of death.

Before we survey some spiritual teachings of the past few millennia, let's first look at the 20th and 21st century and briefly talk about the merger between science and spirituality and some of the implications of this merger. We will first look at how this merger can help us lessen the fear of death and dying.

Death and dying

No book on anxiety would be complete without some discussion on death and the worries it can provoke on a daily basis. At first, I was very hesitant to write about this subject but then I reminded myself of the many individuals with Asperger's I have met who are terrified by the thought of death. Of course, neurotypicals are also not immune to fears about death. Religion helps people of faith deal with the ambiguities of death. For these reasons, I have decided to include this subject in the book, hoping the discussion helps abate people's fears of death.

I suspect the Asperger's population worries about death more intensely than neurotypicals. In a poll taken on www.wrongplanet.net, which asked Aspies how often they think about death and dying in a week, 40 per cent said more than ten times a week (www.wrongplanet.net/postt55551. html). Death represents the ultimate unknown, and people with Asperger's are uncomfortable not knowing what's going to happen next. What could be more unknown than what lies beyond the veil of this existence we call life on earth? It's a question I have thought about for many years.

In trying to approach this subject from an objective point of view, I have looked at the evidence from both sides of the equation. Life either ceases at death and we enter into a void of nothingness (staying "alive" only in the memories of the living), or some part of our essence or soul survives the death of the physical body. In the past 30 to 40 years, I surprisingly discovered science has actually moved to a place where the attempt to tackle this perennial question has gone beyond mere folklore, superstition, and conjecture to a place in which experiential and scientific evidence is mounting.

In my judgment, I believe we survive physical death. Yet whether or not we do is not of paramount importance when it comes to managing present-day anxiety (though for some people, believing in an afterlife lessens the fear of death). Even though I believe the evidence shows death is not the ultimate end of our existence, I'd be lying if I told you I was absolutely certain of that notion. Death happens. Whatever happens to us after we die is beyond our control, and will remain a mystery up until the very end of our lives. This belief, whatever it might be, is something you might need to come to terms with in order to have true peace in your life. What is important to take away from this discussion is to recognize how much your fear of death in the present moment impedes your ability to live a joyous and relaxed life, regardless of what your belief is about what happens at the time of death. If you can manage to overcome a fear of death without a belief in the afterlife, do it.

For the sake of those individuals who think or obsess about death on a daily basis, I'd like to give you some food for thought, if only to quell your worries about something over which you have no control.

Before I present some evidence that indicates our consciousness might survive the demise of the body, let's philosophize about what it would mean. Even if you don't believe in the concept of life after death, I invite you to come along for the ride. How would you feel if there were some form of life after death? Do you think it would make you more or less anxious about the prospect of dying? For many people with Asperger's, the fear of dying might represent a total amelioration of one's individuality or essence. For us Aspies, what seems to matter most is retaining our identity; our sense of who we are. If death is truly the end, then the individuality or essence that defined us would evaporate and become nonexistent at the moment of our last breath. A frightening thought, isn't it?

But what if I were to tell you scientists have been gathering impressive evidence for many years that suggests we do not lose our sense of identity at the time of death? Dr. Raymond Moody, the pioneer of near-death studies, changed the way the world viewed death in his groundbreaking 1975 book, *Life After Life*. This book received the endorsement of pre-eminent death and dying expert and author, Elizabeth Kubler Ross. Moody (1975) reported instances in which individuals who were clinically blind could actually see everything that was taking place in their hospital rooms (and sometimes adjacent rooms) when, by all accounts, they were clinically dead—no heartbeat, flat-lined brain, etc. Amazingly, after these individuals returned from their near-death experiences (NDE) to their bodies, the information they recounted turned out to be correct when verified by hospital staff.

It truly doesn't matter what you believe, as long as you do not let the fear of death control and influence you while you are still alive. If you still believe you will go to heaven based on your religious beliefs and do not want to consider a scientific point of view, that's a good thing if it helps to quell your fears. If you believe the information in this section is absolute nonsense, that's okay too. The mode in which you believe and what you believe is not necessarily important. What is important is the degree to which your fear of death in everyday life impedes your ability to live joyously.

Morphogenetic fields

Before the 1980s, there were no autistic self-advocates lecturing around the world. Temple Grandin was the first to come forth and represent autistic people. Today, there are hundreds of us. Do you think it's a coincidence many others have emerged to speak to and on behalf of autistic people? I don't. In the recorded history of man, no such paradigm existed for autistic self-advocates and yet today, we have many such advocates. How has this group of self-advocates emerged within such a short period of time? One obvious theory is that Temple's emergence, along with a few others, paved the way for people on the autism spectrum to have the confidence to advocate their interests on a broader scale. One could argue that no one had ever heard of autism before this century, so it only makes sense more of us are emerging. These are certainly plausible enough theories. But the fact that Temple Grandin, Thomas McKean, Donna Williams, and others came on the scene within a few years of each other indicates something else was taking place. If we dig a little and investigate this amazing emergence of powerful voices within the autistic community, we can find some meaningful and intellectually satisfying answers.

There is a considerable body of scientific evidence suggesting there is a unifying field underlying everyday reality (James 2007). Quantum physics, which is one of our most reliable sciences, shows us that on a subatomic level, everything is interconnected. Alan Aspect conclusively proved what Bell's theorem (John Stewart Bell) theoretically posited earlier: if you take a pair of twin photons and send them to opposite ends of the universe, each twin will seem to know what the other one is doing. The question many people have asked in the last several decades is whether the principles of the subatomic world apply to the world of matter. We know photons have the capacity to stay instantaneously connected over long distances, but is that true for objects? How about for humans?

In the 1980s, Cambridge University biologist Rupert Sheldrake wrote *A New Science of Life*, a groundbreaking book (1981) in which he put forth a hypothesis known as the "hypothesis of formative causation" or "morphogenetic fields", which presents evidence that some sort of invisible force is at work in the universe. When the book was published, some people said the book should be burned because the implications of his theory were completely revolutionary and disrupted the prevailing notions of the scientific establishment. Sheldrake postulated the evolution of the universe is like the evolution of nature—there are no eternal laws, only habitual tendencies. A chick hatches in a certain way only because the process of hatching has taken place on a grand scale over time. It has become a habitual process. When a dog learns a trick for the first time that no dog has ever mastered, theoretically, dogs around the world should have an easier time learning the trick, if only on a very small scale. However, if enough dogs learn this new trick over many years, the trick should become inborn, like telling your dog to "sit" or "roll over." Did you ever wonder why it is relatively easy for dogs to learn certain tricks and not others? It's almost like they were born with the capacity to know how to sit, roll over, and shake hands on command. However, try to teach a dog to walk on its hind legs, and that would be a more difficult task. This may sound like nonsense, but consider the following:

1. Experimental psychologist and theorist William McDougall (Harman 1998) conducted experiments on rats and found training could be inherited from one generation to the next.

2. On the Japanese island of Koshima, monkeys very slowly learned how to wash potatoes, apparently a new behavior for the species. Researchers observed once a critical number of monkeys was reached—the so-called hundredth monkey—this previously learned behavior instantly spread across the water to monkeys on nearby islands. This became known as the Hundredth Monkey Phenomenon.

3. Dr. Arden Mahlberg created a false Morse code that wasn't any easier or harder to learn than the real Morse code. Not knowing which one was authentic, subjects learned the real one faster (Sherwood 2002).

4. Yale psychologist Gary Schwartz tested a group of 90 students who did not know the Hebrew alphabet. He showed them 96 words, half real and half false, but the words sounded identical. Participants (who did not know half the words were false) responded twice as confidently when viewing the real words than when viewing the scrambled words (Sheldrake 1995).

5. It is not uncommon for two people to come up with the exact same invention or idea independently of each other and within a relatively short period of time (Robbins 1997) when that idea had never previously been considered throughout recorded human history.

6. In the 1920s in a localized area in Southampton, England, a bird called the blue tit discovered it could tear off the tops of milk bottles (on doorsteps) and drink the cream (Wolfe 1998). Shortly thereafter, the same phenomenon was reported over 100 miles away. But blue tits never fly more than 15 miles from their home and live only two or three years. Suddenly, this behavior was reported in Denmark, Germany, and throughout Great Britain when it had never happened before. How was this possible?

If Sheldrake's theory is true, it has dramatic implications. Consider this: when you, as a person with Asperger's, learn to control your own anxiety, you may be indirectly helping others with Asperger's. It's exciting to consider the ramifications of morphogenetic fields. To think that you and I might possess the power to influence others beyond our scope is overwhelming. Yet look at what has happened during the past 20 years within the autistic advocacy movement. Not long ago, there was no such thing as an autistic culture. However, it emerged in a cosmic blink. In the same way, when you control and master your anxiety, you may be participating in a similar kind of experience, similar to what Carl Jung referred to when he coined the term "collective unconscious". Except according to Sheldrake's theory, the influence you have will be greatest among people with whom you have the most self-similarity. This makes sense. A dog will probably have more influence over other dogs than he will over cats. Sheldrake's theory implies not only will controlling your own anxiety be a beneficial aspect of your own life, but you may be indirectly helping other people with Asperger's on a very subtle level to accomplish the same feat. Talk about power! Whether the existence of this power is real or illusory, it raises an interesting premise to ponder.

Viktor Frankl

What could possibly be more harrowing than being imprisoned in a Nazi concentration camp? Surely, someone who survived that experience would have something significant to say about anxiety and stress management. Existential psychotherapist Viktor Frankl (1959) wrote *Man's Search for Meaning,* a powerful book about his experience as a survivor of a concentration camp during the Holocaust. In vivid detail, Frankl describes being treated like an animal and seeing those around him receive the same treatment and worse, including mass slaughter. With the precariousness of life standing in the balance on a daily basis, Frankl turned inward. In the midst of these unimaginable circumstances, he found an inner peace that insulated him from his brutal external environment. He connected with his spirit and found a glowing love radiating from his core. Can you imagine being in Auschwitz and not even knowing whether your spouse was alive or dead? Those were the circumstances facing Frankl. Impending death and inhumane treatment on a daily basis were not enough to destroy his inner spirit.

Most of us will never have to experience anything as terrifying as what Viktor Frankl had to endure. Yet, look at how he handled the situation. Under the circumstances, Frankl's fear of death may have lessened in the face of constant terror. *Overcoming the fear of death, he was also able to conquer life.* He proved no amount of living hell could make him succumb and give up his inner spirit. Being a Holocaust survivor probably gave Frankl the inner wisdom to become one of the most influential thinkers and writers of the twentieth century. I have little doubt he would not have attained this status without having lived through this terrible experience in Auschwitz. He was able to give his life meaning under circumstances far worse than any of us face in our lives today.

Anxiety and freedom

The existential philosopher Kierkegaard (Gerzon 1997) remarked that anxiety is a byproduct of human freedom. Looking at it from this existential point of view, perhaps Frankl was able to actualize his inner spirit because his freedom was denied. He had no real options to actualize himself in society, or at least so it seemed at the time. This may explain why prisoners turn to religion and find a sense of inner peace they weren't able to find in their lives beyond the prison walls. Freedom and choice do create anxiety. Our lives are full of potential when we are born. How we utilize that potential is a choice. If our lives were scripted for us and we merely read the script, life wouldn't be very stressful. We would be playing out our predestined roles, scripted consequences and all. Because we have free will, we have the potential to make mistakes or what I would rather label, "learning opportunities".

Kierkegaard said anxiety is a challenge (Gerzon 1997). I interpret that to mean this: The greater the anxiety, the more opportunity there is for growth. Looking at it this way, we should be grateful we have the opportunity to face our fears during our lifetime. In the movie *Defending Your Life,* Albert Brooks portrays Daniel Miller, who dies in an automobile crash and goes to a purgatory called "Judgment City". It is there he is required to defend his life. He must prove in a courtroom-style process that he successfully overcame his fears. If his judges find he didn't make the most of that life, he will be sent back to earth to try again and again until he gets it right. If he can prove he overcame his fears, he merits moving up to "citizen of the universe".

This movie is a great metaphor for life. I believe the more anxiety you face and conquer in your lifetime, the greater your spiritual growth will be. If you look at the historic figures we admire, they didn't sit around watching TV and eating snack food. They took risks, exposed themselves to criticism, and faced their fears.

Animals and fear

There is a great line from the Koran, "How many animals do not carry their own provision! God provides for them and for you. He is Alert, Aware." The next time you have an opportunity to watch a dog at play, or a school of fish swimming, or a cat climbing a tree, you will observe animals are engaged in the present moment. To them, past and future simply do not exist. They're not worried about dying, where they will get their next meal, or whether they'll receive a promotion. The only fear animals experience is when it is present-moment fear—when predators are chasing them or when one of their young is hurt. They do not fear the future or lament the past.

We can learn from our animal friends in this regard. If animals could talk to us, it would be interesting to know if they could conceptualize fear and anxiety beyond the present. My guess is they can't. It's a foreign concept to them. Ironically, there are parallels between animal thought processes and the philosophy of Viktor Frankl:

1. Both are/were fully engaged by the present moment.

2. Both are/were fully detached from the past and future.

Becoming more like Frankl

So how do we become more like our animal friends and Viktor Frankl? The answer to this question is by embracing our freedom and recognizing we are in a learning environment. Let me explain.

I'm sure you can remember an unpleasant and anxiety-provoking dream that seemed so real to you when you woke up, you had to acknowledge it was only a dream. Maybe it was a dream prompting you to think about something important that could be incorporated into your waking life. Nevertheless, it was still just a dream.

Our lives operate in a similar fashion. We live in a sort of earth school (Zukav 1989) where we get to learn about and practice controlling our anxiety. While we're alive, everything seems so real, so permanent (like the dream state), but what if we were to approach life as if it were a laboratory? In this life laboratory, we have the freedom to explore, play, and make some mistakes (and not be judged for any of it). When all is said and done, we return to a realm to evaluate how we did without wrathful judgment. I urge you to imagine life this way, if only for 24 hours. Viewing it from this perspective, it won't seem so daunting. We don't have to take ourselves so seriously.

By embracing freedom and recognizing we are in a learning environment, we get the best of both worlds. Instead of fearing mistakes, we begin to see opportunities for growth. Instead of fearing anxiety, we begin to look for opportunities to conquer it.

Looking at life from this perspective, you become the brave warrior I spoke of in Chapter 2. By embracing freedom and accepting the consequences of your actions, you accelerate your spiritual growth. Resisting the curriculum of life has the opposite effect on your spiritual growth.

Buddhism and attachments

We spoke about the noble truths of Buddhism. The Buddhist way of life has much to teach us when it comes to managing anxiety. By studying a particular teaching of Buddhism, we can even make some connections to cognitive-behavioral therapy. For the purpose of our discussion, I would like to focus on one key aspect of the Buddhist teachings: attachments.

In Chapter 8, which discussed meltdowns, I referred to the earthly goal of becoming free of attachments. This includes material attachments, unwanted thoughts, status, gratification, etc. When one is focused on these attachments, it's easy to see how cognitive distortions and early maladaptive schemas can come into play. Early maladaptive schemas and core beliefs imply there is something lacking. A core belief holds you up to an artificial standard you set for yourself. "I should be _____ and because I'm not, it means I'm _____." From a Buddhist point of view, the negative core beliefs you have formed about yourself are a result of the attachments you have to earthly status. By focusing on what you should or shouldn't be and what society expects of you, you are actually clinging to what gratifies your ego. You may also be clinging to your cognitive distortions or unwanted and intrusive thoughts that don't meet your authentic emotional needs. When you can move beyond your ego (the false sense of self) into a more heightened state of awareness, you'll begin to see the theoretical attainment of earthly status won't make you less anxious. Why? Because you'll always be afraid you can lose what you've attained, and you'll always want more of what you've attained. You'll never be satisfied.

When you can let go of your attachments, you free yourself. The attachments do not rule you anymore. Your life no longer depends on attaining them. When you drop the expectations that you, your family, or society places on you and let go of approval attachments, it becomes easier to enjoy life. I've had to learn this lesson many different ways throughout my life thus far.

Please do not misunderstand me. I'm not saying you shouldn't strive for success in life. What I am saying is the beliefs you have about yourself should not be dependent upon the outside world. I'm sure you've heard it said that happiness comes from within, and it's true. *When you can be content under the most dire circumstances (like Frankl), you are no longer dependent on the outside world to affirm your identity. You already know who you are.* Once you come to this realization, you have conquered life. That's the secret, right there.

Again, look at Viktor Frankl. Someone was constantly degrading him. However, the experiences did not destroy the foundation of Frankl's core identity because he knew who he was. He didn't need the approval of others to reinforce his self-worth. Instead of the concentration camp experience destroying his will to live, it heightened his self-esteem and gave him the inner strength to survive.

Christianity and faith

In general, I observe life through my left-brain functioning and an objective assessment of the evidence at hand, but Christianity has taught me something about the value of faith. In Christianity, putting one's faith in Jesus Christ means you will enter the Kingdom of Heaven upon the death of your physical body. Along those lines, I have found a great deal of value in putting my faith in the universe. I think faith is an important factor in leading a less anxious life. According to an article on www.webmd.com, religious people tend to live longer, healthier lives than non-religious people, presumably, because faith provides a positive outlook and the social benefits of being involved in a religious community (www.webmd.com/news/20000809/religious-people-live-longer-than-nonbelievers).

One must have a degree of faith considering the many complex processes occurring simultaneously in life. Your body operates like a complex and sophisticated machine, simultaneously performing an infinite number of tasks in a magnificent manner. At this very moment, every cell in your body is engaging in multiple tasks. Just think of it, trillions of cells each carrying out different and important functions at the same time. Not only are you not aware of these ongoing processes, but you aren't in the least bit worried about this part of your inner biology. You believe in your body's innate intelligence to get the job done. You don't know for a fact everything is happening as it should. For all you know, there could be a cancerous patch of cells growing somewhere. When you go to sleep, you willingly lose consciousness believing you will wake up the next morning. Yet, you have faith your body is doing what it should.

The attitude we take toward our bodies and the cosmos (knowing the sun will rise in the east) is a healthy one. When we have a basic faith life is as it should be, we tend to adopt an attitude of stoicism and peace. You've probably heard the Serenity Prayer, but it bears repeating, "God, grant me the serenity to accept the things I cannot change; the courage to change the things I can; and the wisdom to know the difference."

Judaism and interconnectedness

I'm Jewish, but know next to nothing about my religion. I am not qualified to weave together spiritual teachings from Judaism into a discussion on how individuals with Asperger's can control their anxiety. What I can do, however, is talk about something I've learned from growing up in a Jewish culture.

I live in metropolitan Detroit, which has quite a large Jewish population. Yet, it strangely appears as if all the Jewish people who live in this area know one another. The interconnectedness among Jewish people (at least where I live) is extraordinarily tight. The population understands it has an obligation—beyond individual needs—to identify and serve the needs of others. Taking it a step further, Jewish people seem to understand the spiritual principle of interconnectedness: that at some level, everything in the universe is one.

To believe you are one with the universe can alter your perception of life. Theoretically, if I am a part of you and you are a part of me, then we all share some important common concerns. Suddenly, your worries are no longer individual concerns. It becomes clearer humanity exists as one global body, and all of us are like cells in that body. Similarly, thoughts that are purely egocentric create inner anxiety if they have been reinforced into negative distortions, beliefs, or schemas. Being mindful you are participating in a global drama as well as your own, you'll begin to enlarge your perspective. Suddenly, the smaller worries you might have had begin to dissipate when you focus on the larger picture.

The final word

I would like to suggest that, by having Asperger's, many of us are forced to conquer more anxiety in our lifetimes than we could have ever anticipated. Just by having Asperger's, we have a host of challenges others do not have to face. *But if spiritual growth happens by facing your fears and conquering them, this conceivably means people with greater challenges in life can also attain the greatest spiritual growth.* If you were born into a multi-billion dollar home where you never had to work a single day in your life, how much spiritual growth would you achieve? I am sure of three things:

1. More freedom and choice in life leads to more anxiety.

2. More challenges in life also lead to more anxiety.

3. Challenges and freedom are good things. Embrace them, face them, and you will grow spiritually.

By realizing our lives are nothing more than a simulation, a playground, a laboratory where we permit ourselves to make mistakes within a safe framework, we can learn to relax about life and not be so anxious. Fellow Aspies: we have the freedom to make choices regarding our lives. We haven't been dealt the easiest hand in life, but challenges and freedom are what ultimately lead to spiritual growth. Are you ready to be free? Are you ready to face those challenges? If so, welcome. You have begun an incredible journey.

Action points

- Viktor Frankl demonstrated it is possible to stay connected to one's inner spirit, despite the worst circumstances. Learn from his example.

- Animals are highly spiritual beings because they live life in the present moment. Learn from their example.

- To conquer anxiety, accept your freedom, view life like an earth school, and accept nothing lasts forever.

Epilogue

I have tried to convey my knowledge of anxiety and Asperger's from a firsthand point of view and from my perspective as a doctoral student in psychology. I have been working on controlling my anxiety all of my adult life. I've tried to absorb as much information that has been available on the subject and have then tried my best to integrate that information into my understanding of Asperger syndrome.

I hope what you take away from reading this book is the sense that you are in greater control of your destiny than you otherwise thought. I have empathized with how difficult and unpredictable the world is for someone with Asperger's and how that can cause anxiety. I have also tried to instill the notion that the choice to control your own anxiety is entirely yours. The task of controlling your anxiety is a real challenge but one worth taking.

One thing that may differentiate this book from other books you have read about Asperger's is much of my attention has focused on your inner processes versus the conditions of the external world. Admittedly, there are no quick fixes or easy answers, but I sincerely hope this book has helped you get to know yourself a little better. My primary goal was for you to gain better self-awareness. When you have insight into yourself, you can make better choices. By making better choices, you can curtail much of your unwanted anxiety.

Try to apply the information from this book into your life one chapter at a time. Each chapter offers several different strategies for you to consider.

I have spent the last four years in admiration of what the Asperger's population is capable of achieving. It never ceases to amaze me when I read a new book by an author with Asperger's, or see someone with Asperger's give a dynamic presentation at a conference, or watch brave leaders with Asperger's who are part of the neurodiversity movement. I've always sensed there is something special about individuals with Asperger syndrome and have never met a person with Asperger's who I didn't find interesting in some significant way. We each have gifts to offer the world and fear can often be the barrier that holds us back from reaching our potential.

Look at the neurodiversity movement, spearheaded by a group of passionate individuals on the autism spectrum who believe autistics should be accepted as being different but not defective. They rail against groups of individuals who speak of a cure and are equally passionate to help other individuals with autism spectrum disorders (or differences, as they put it) reach their potential. Whether or not you agree with what these individuals are trying to do, you have to admire their courage in attaining their goal. Instead of being complacent, they are taking on some of the most influential autism organizations in the world, facing the possibility of alienating people within the autism spectrum. Their bravery reflects their strong belief in their cause. These individuals have done a lot of self-development, preparing themselves for an onslaught of criticism. People with autism are supposed to have social disabilities, yet these leaders are organizing grassroots efforts to try to change the perceptions worldwide about people with autism.

Others with autism and Asperger's write books and speak at local and national conferences. I am one of those people. One needs to have worked through a great deal of anxiety to be doing this kind of work. The rewards couldn't be sweeter—helping others and helping oneself (finding an exciting and challenging career path and controlling and mastering anxiety).

I am not suggesting you have to become an autism self-advocate to conquer your anxieties, but by following your passions, you will likely have to step outside your comfort zone. To do what you really want to do in life and not have your fears get in the way, you will have to take risks. The good news is others on the spectrum have walked this path and taken these risks. They have stepped outside their comfort zones and as a result, autistics throughout the world are now being heard. As I once heard Michael John Carley say at a presentation, "People with autism have gone from being the zoo exhibits to the zoologists."

Even though people with Asperger's have great potential, we often do not realize our talents to their fullest degree. This creates a certain amount of existential anxiety for many people with Asperger's, who strongly believe they have a purpose in life but can't quite figure out how to express their gifts. They know they have something special to offer but aren't sure how to go about it. Does this sound like you? Without sounding simplistic, I want to say, fellow Aspies: I believe in you. I believe in your potential. I believe with enough hard work, you will break down the barriers that hold you back. Eventually, you will find your way in this world. The first prerequisite to make this goal a reality is to reduce your anxiety.

I have met too many individuals with Asperger's who are trapped by fear. They are paralyzed in their own self-imposed prison to which only they have the key. I've often felt if I could help reduce the anxiety these people experience, they would be able to discover their passions can lead to great things. I've sensed it deeply, and that's why I wrote this book.

All your life, people have told you what you couldn't do, that you have a lot of shortcomings and disabilities. In this book, I've tried to encourage you to define yourself and not let others limit your vision. In school, teachers probably belittled you about causing problems and disappointing people who were trying to help you. Maybe your siblings grew frustrated with having a brother or sister with special needs who took up so much of the family's attention. You've acquired a lot of guilt, shame, and anxiety from these messages, but the fact you are reading this book means you haven't given up. You're still in the process of working through these issues. I believe once you are able to make some progress on the emotions that are self-limiting, good things will begin to happen in your life. You will be able to tap into a dormant talent you have never utilized. You'll begin to accept yourself for who you are, social foibles and all. You'll be able to compensate consciously for your weaknesses by building on your strengths. My wish for you is once the fear and anxiety starts to decrease, your true potential will begin to soar.

The best way to understand how your anxiety has played a role in your life is to meet other people with Asperger's and talk to them about their experiences. Though your levels of fear won't be identical, you'll begin to understand that you aren't alone. There are others like you who have similar fears for similar reasons; those who think they are defective because that's what they were taught to believe; those who feel frustrated they are not utilizing their talents. I encourage you to go online and look for sites in which individuals with Asperger's gather and share their feelings about these issues.

As you begin to see you are not alone, this affirmation should give you strength. Michael John Carley (2008) points out one of the major benefits of receiving an Asperger's diagnosis in adulthood is becoming part of a community. People finally understand they are not deficient, but, rather, there are neurological reasons to explain their behavioral differences. There is the realization that meltdowns happened for a reason and maybe even served a constructive purpose. Those intense fears occurred not because you were emotionally impaired but because of how your system was wired. Through friendships with others who have lived similar experiences, you begin to dissolve the shame, which is often the origin of our fears. By normalizing who you are and putting yourself within the context of a larger group of people with whom you have common interests, you effectively minimize the self-blame that's haunted you throughout most of your life.

Be proud of belonging to a creative and innovative group of people. Not everyone with Asperger's is a genius, but we are unique and have talents and abilities many neurotypicals wish they possessed. Be proud of who you are, and you'll find there is less to be anxious about in your life. The more self-acceptance and confidence you display, the less you'll project your fears onto the world.

If you dream about going back to college but have made excuses why you can't, pinpoint what's holding you back, and make your dream a reality. Don't let fear stop you. If you've wanted to meet new people socially but aren't sure whether you can be successful, do it anyway. Don't let fear stop you. If you have thought about joining a club where other people with Asperger's meet, but part of you is ashamed of the diagnosis, don't let fear stop you. If you've wanted to apply for a particular position but question whether you can handle the responsibilities, don't let fear stop you. If you have decided it's time to leave your parents' home but aren't sure about giving up the security of living with them, don't let fear stop you. If you dream about speaking at an autism conference but don't think you have enough confidence, don't let fear stop you.

As a person with Asperger's, you have the ability to affect the world and make a meaningful difference in people's lives, just by virtue of your unique talents. That will never happen if you let fear hold you back. I challenge you to challenge whatever doubts you have about yourself through the practice of CBT. Think twice the next time you let fear stand between you and your dreams. However your self-concept has developed and limited your expectations of life, you have the power to change your self-image starting *now*. By helping those with Asperger's to actualize their potential, I believe I am making the world a better place in which to live. If just one reader is able to transcend his or her shame, fear, or doubt, after having read this book, I will consider it a success.

Appendix I

An interview with my parents

In this appendix, I want to give you (the reader) an opportunity to hear from the two people who know me best: my mother and father. I asked them a series of questions relating to my own development and stress management skills, from their perspective. The following is their (Larry and Kitty Dubin's) unedited accounts:

Nick: At what age did you notice my anxiety begin to intensify where it started to interfere with daily functioning?

Mom: When you were about four, I remember going to Mother-Toddler groups with you. We played games like "Ring Around The Rosy" and "Duck, Duck, Goose" and often, you wouldn't join in the circle. At the time, I didn't think of that behavior as anxiety, but in retrospect, it certainly was. There were other situations where you would separate yourself from the group, for example, when playing at a park or being at the beach where other children were present. You would frequently choose to play by yourself rather than join the group.

I also remember, as early as first grade, when children were starting to call each other on the phone to play. That was something that created a lot of anxiety for you. You always seemed happy when someone called you, but initiating the call was extremely difficult. I can think of many times when you would pace around the phone, trying to get up the nerve to call someone and then you would just give up in defeat.

As you got older, being part of a social group was something that made you highly anxious. Examples that come to mind are: attending school dances, going to school football games, and being part of the teen group at our temple. You either refused to participate or did so under great duress. These were situations you and I fought about *before* your diagnosis. I thought you were just being obstinate in not wanting to go. I had no idea how difficult these situations were for you, and also how little interest you genuinely had in them. I would advise any parent of a child with Asperger's *not* to put pressure on their child to do something they don't want to do or that makes them uncomfortable. A parent may think he or she is doing what's best for the child, but chances are it's what would make the parent feel better.

When you went away to college, living in the dorm proved intolerable for you. You simply could not deal with the intensely social milieu of dorm life. The loud noises and living in a small space with another person created such anxiety that you said you wanted to leave college and come back home. It was an ongoing battle to keep you in college your freshman year and you wound up having to move out of the dorm into a rooming house in order to stay there.

Besides social situations, another source of anxiety was when you had to "change gears" or make some kind of transition. For example, it was very difficult for you to go back to school after being on a vacation. Also, dealing with unexpected events would send you into an anxious state. I remember one night when you were away at college, there was a big storm and the power went out in the dorm. You became extremely upset and felt it necessary to leave the dorm and spend the night in a hotel. It was an unexpected situation and you were really "freaked out" by it.

Dad: When you were about four or five, you would become very anxious about being in social situations. Being invited to another child's birthday party would not be something you would want to do. You would worry about it. If the party had a theme requiring a skill that you were not good at (e.g. gymnastics or ice skating), you became very anxious.

You were much more at ease having a play date with one other child. The party environment was more problematic because you had to socialize with many children at the same time.

It became very clear as you got older that social situations made you nervous. You were afraid of not being liked and would withdraw in these situations. Looking back, it is easy to understand your mindset. You could sense that you were different from other children. You wanted to be liked but didn't know how to make it happen.

Nick: Was there a time that you can remember where I wasn't anxious?

Mom: Before ages 3 to 4, I didn't perceive you as anxious. I saw you more as being "hyper" and having an excessive amount of energy.

Dad: You have never been what I would call laid back. You've always been intense and strong-willed. That is just the way you are wired. However, you did seem to relax when we went on vacation, and you didn't have to face the demands of school and the pressures of getting along with other children. Every summer we would go to Sleepy Hollow, a resort on Lake Michigan. You loved going there. You loved to swim, play tennis, and even do arts and crafts. The anxiety would just melt away.

Nick: From a parental perspective, what do you think have been the main causes of my anxiety?

Mom: I don't know if I'd use the word "causes". I would say that there were/are certain situations that trigger anxiety and there are also ways of thinking that create anxiety.

- Ways of thinking that created anxiety for you:
  1. Black and white thinking—things are either good or bad.
  2. Perfectionism—feeling you have to do things perfectly and that you can never make a mistake.
- Situations that triggered anxiety for you:
  1. Making transitions.
  2. Being in a situation where others are evaluating you.

3. Dealing with the unexpected.

4. Parties.

Dad: You have always sensed that you were different. This awareness created anxiety because you didn't really understand why you were different and you also tried not to be different. Unfortunately, you did not get any understanding about all this until you were 27 and were diagnosed with Asperger's.

One way that you would try to compensate for feeling different was to be the best at any activity in which you would participate. For example, when you started playing tennis and saw that you had some talent for the sport, you weren't content until you became the best tennis player on your school team and won a number of tournaments. You played the top spot (number one singles) on your high school and college tennis teams which helped compensate for feeling deficient in other areas. It was your way of gaining the respect and admiration of others.

Having to be the best at anything naturally produces a lot of anxiety. Instead of just enjoying an activity or a sport, you needed to gain attention for doing well. If you sensed you weren't going to be good at some activity, you weren't even willing to try it.

Nick: In your view, how has Asperger's played a role in making me more anxious?

Mom: I think Asperger's increases anxiety in the following ways: Because of the tendency towards black and white thinking, if there was a situation where you made even a small "mistake" or didn't do something perfectly, that would create anxiety. Black and white thinking also interfered with how you viewed some other people in your life. If a friend, a coach or a teacher unintentionally did something to hurt your feelings, you were ready to end the relationship. It took a long time for you to see that things were more "gray" than black and white, in terms of evaluating yourself, other people, and life in general.

Dad: Asperger syndrome is of neurological origin that consists of many different characteristics. Some of these characteristics provide strengths as well as challenges. You have benefited from having strengths that can be attributed to Asperger's (i.e.) powers of concentration, good memory, creativity, honesty, individuality, strong verbal skills, and acquisition of knowledge in areas of special interest. You have also faced many challenges as a result of having Asperger's. You have had to struggle socially, coped with learning difficulties, and you have had to work hard to gain self-confidence.

Nick: Was there any positive benefit to my high anxiety that you can think of?

Mom: As with all anxious people, it probably made you more vigilant about anticipating things that could go wrong and preparing for them. Also, being anxious makes you always be on time.

Dad: The main benefit that comes to mind is that your anxiety seems to fuel your passions.

Nick: Have you noticed me becoming less anxious over the years? If so, what specific differences have you noticed?

Mom: Absolutely! There has been tremendous progress over the years. First, you are better able to tolerate imperfection in yourself as well as in others. As you've grown older, you have been able to see that people rarely do anything perfectly and so now, you judge yourself less harshly than you previously did. If you "make a mistake" you don't focus solely on the mistake, like you used to. You are more apt to see the big picture. You also cut others more slack when they do something wrong. It is no longer grounds for ending a relationship. You have learned that even people you love and who love you can do something that hurts or angers you.

Your level of frustration tolerance has also decreased. I can remember a time when being in a traffic jam would have made you very anxious, but now it doesn't. You roll with the punches more now than you ever did. This growth is especially evident with all the traveling you do. By nature, traveling is filled with unexpected situations and potential frustrations. When these things occur, such as travel delays or other mishaps, you seem to take them in stride and not get ruffled by them.

I see you as someone who has made great progress in dealing with anxiety. I think a lot of that has to do with self-awareness. You know what situations trigger anxiety and you also know certain attitudes that can create anxiety. So much of your anxiety in the past was "unconscious". You have much more control over your emotions now.

Dad: You have become a totally different person. You are much less anxious and more willing to challenge yourself with new experiences. You have accepted your Asperger's diagnosis in a positive way. The diagnosis has helped you to better understand yourself. This self-knowledge has made you more comfortable with both your strengths and weaknesses. You no longer blame yourself for your weaknesses and you don't focus on them. You appreciate your strengths, and in the process, have become less anxious and depressed.

Nick: As the parent of someone with ASD, what would you personally recommend to someone with Asperger's who is looking to manage their stress more effectively?

Mom: I think cognitive-behavioral therapy is very useful for someone with Asperger's. In this particular kind of therapy, a person's way of thinking is challenged and explored. If someone evaluates himself in terms of black and white thinking, he almost always comes out badly. This way of thinking creates a kind of perfectionism that is impossible to live up to. A behavioral therapist could also provide strategies for dealing with unexpected events and making transitions.

Personally, I am a big journal keeper. I think recording and keeping track of situations that create anxiety is a good idea. It helps give you increased awareness of your own patterns and how to deal with them more effectively. So—I would suggest that a person with Asperger's keep a daily Anxiety Journal. Identify what ways of thinking and what particular situations create anxiety for you. If you are in therapy, it would make sessions more effective because you would have specifics to work on and talk about, rather than dealing in generalities.

I would add couple of things parents can do:

1. Do not put pressure on your child to participate in activities or events in which they have no interest and will create undue anxiety.

2. Engage in a lot of discussion with your child. Help him or her process situations in which they might be using black or white thinking or perfectionism to evaluate themselves. Show them that there is a whole "gray area" to life and that there are other options besides being perfect or being bad.

Dad: Accept your diagnosis as a gift. See it as a way to gain a great amount of self-knowledge. Assess all of the strengths that you have as a result of the diagnosis. Determine how you can use those strengths to your advantage. Seek the necessary support (e,g. counselors, psychologists, coaches, tutors) to help you cope with the difficulties you encounter in life. Develop your special interests and try, if possible, to have them serve as a basis for further educational studies and possible future employment.

Recommended Books

Feeling Good by David Burns
This book is what I consider to be the best introduction to cognitive-behavioral therapy techniques that one can use on him or herself, written specifically for the layperson in mind.

Emotional Alchemy by Tara Bennett-Goleman
This book presents the reader with a Buddhist approach at examining emotions through the process at looking at one's schemas.

Emotional Intelligence by Daniel Goleman
Written by Tara's husband Daniel, this book helps one understand the biological basis for his or her emotions and how they can be consciously controlled.

How to Control Anxiety Before it Controls You by Albert Ellis
Readers of this book with Asperger syndrome will probably appreciate Ellis's straightforward and candid writing style. Ellis is one of the pioneers of CBT and developed an offshoot of it called rational emotive behavior therapy.

The Power of Now by Eckhart Tolle

Tolle helps the reader realize the power of not letting the past or the future create unnecessary anxiety in the present moment.

The Complete Guide to Asperger's Syndrome by Tony Attwood

The "bible" of Asperger's syndrome and a great resource to help someone with Asperger's gain self-understanding.

Asperger's from the Inside Out by Michael John Carley

The best guidebook for a newly diagnosed adult with Asperger syndrome, bar-none!

Reinventing your Life by Jeffery Young and Janet Kloso

From the creators of schema therapy, this book offers the reader a very accessible and practical guide towards uncovering and replacing outdated schemas, or "lifetraps".

Cognitive Behavioral Therapy for Adult Asperger Syndrome by Valerie Gaus

Even though the primary audience for this book is professionals who work with ASD individuals, readers with Asperger's who want to expand their knowledge of CBT and how it applies to our population will find this book extremely useful.

Appendix III

Aspie self-checklist

After I received my diagnosis back in 2004, I made a list of the various Asperger traits that I felt characterized who I was. How many of these traits do you share with me?

> These characteristics listed below are simply Asperger traits that I (Nick Dubin) display and by no means represent a clinical basis for a diagnosis of Asperger's. To be sure of any diagnosis, contact a mental health practitioner.

General

- ☐ 1. I feel incompatible with the culture I was born into. I feel culturally "illiterate", that is, I do not know what movies are currently showing and do not really care. I do not like the current pop music of the day. My musical tastes are different from most people my age.

- ☐ 2. I often feel that if I cannot be the best at what I attempt, I shouldn't attempt it at all.

- ☐ 3. Multitasking (or doing many things at the same time) is almost impossible for me.

☐ 4. I crave positions of control and responsibility because I hate being told what to do, but I worry that I do not have the necessary abilities to handle such a job of authority.

☐ 5. Authenticity is vitally important to me.

☐ 6. The idea of a menial job where I cannot express my creativity is revolting to me.

☐ 7. I have certain political, world or social views that are well outside the mainstream.

☐ 8. If I'm going to do a job, I get the job done right, although it might be slower than expected.

☐ 9. I cannot start another project until I finish the one I am currently working on.

☐ 10. As a baby, younger child and even today, I was and am especially finicky about certain foods.

☐ 11. I am a perfectionist.

☐ 12. I find dates (calendars) to be fascinating. I like to know when things occurred.

☐ 13. I am fascinated with how things change over time.

☐ 14. I usually have a "one track mind".

☐ 15. I often lack "common sense" when it comes to everyday tasks that seem easy for others.

☐ 16. I have a problem "seeing the forest for the trees", or understanding what is important and what is not.

☐ 17. I have difficulty generalizing information from one experience to another.

☐ 18. Even though I have high standards for people, I often tend to trust too easily.

☐ 19. I am not a rule breaker, regardless of the situation.

☐ 20. I am one of the most ethical moral people I know.

☐ 21. In the past, I have been diagnosed with either classic autism, a general learning disability, schizoid personality disorder, schizophrenia, attention deficit hyperactivity disorder, obsessive compulsive disorder, post-traumatic stress syndrome, general depression, semantic pragmatic disorder, PDD-NOS, Tourette's syndrome, sensory integration dysfunction, nonverbal learning disability, hyperlexia, or dyspraxia.

☐ 22. A member of my immediate family has been diagnosed with an autism spectrum disorder (or one of the other diagnoses listed above).

Emotions

☐ 23. I am serious most of the time. People have often told me to "lighten up".

☐ 24. After a long day of expending energy, I need lots of downtime.

☐ 25. I have a temper that can come out at unexpected times.

☐ 26. I need things to be a certain way, and I will literally go into a meltdown state if they are not the way I want them. Relatively small problems throughout the course of a day can send me into a meltdown state. For example, a flat tire, flight delays at the airport, a restaurant being out of a certain food, etc.

☐ 27. I hate transitions throughout the course of a day.

☐ 28. I dislike unpredictability. I *like* order and structure, and often *need* it.

☐ 29. I often feel that there is a huge dichotomy within myself because although I consider myself creative, I am extremely rigid.

☐ 30. If I do not show empathy, I feel it is not because I do not want to be empathetic, but it's genuinely because I missed an important piece of information.

☐ 31. Perhaps nothing makes me angrier than seeing injustice.

☐ 32. Separating from my parents was or is a very difficult thing for me.

☐ 33. My childhood went by too quickly. I do not feel ready to tackle the "real world".

☐ 34. I do not like the idea of drinking alcohol or taking drugs because I want to be in control of my own behavior. I do not like the idea of being controlled by any substance.

☐ 35. I would hate to be hypnotized because the idea of someone controlling my behavior is unacceptable.

Academics

☐ 36. As a child, I found the activities in school, such as handwriting, art, and physical education very laborious.

☐ 37. In school, I tended to tune out what I was not interested in.

☐ 38. I received some special education services as a child.

☐ 39. I attended a university. If not, I would want to be able to.

☐ 40. I am more of a thinker than a feeler.

☐ 41. I tend to be a visual learner.

☐ 42. I tend to have trouble with visual-spatial processing.

☐ 43. I consider myself extremely intelligent.

☐ 44. I pride myself on what I know... not on who I know.

☐ 45. I often feel like the "comeback kid" in that I learn things a bit later than others, but once I do, I embrace it fully.

Language/speech/processing

☐ 46. I find it difficult to pick up the general theme or plot of most movies I watch.

☐ 47. It takes me a few seconds to process what the other person has said before I can give a meaningful response. This is often frustrating for me because it seems like others can respond much more quickly than I can.

☐ 48. As a child, I had a speech delay that quickly caught up to age appropriate levels.

☐ 49. I rarely lie, and if I do, it is extremely uncomfortable.

☐ 50. I do not understand the point of "small talk".

☐ 51. I have a large vocabulary and tend to use big words during informal conversations, and/or as a child, I sounded like a "little professor" because I was so articulate for my age.

☐ 52. I have a sense of humor, but it is different from most people. I find puns and word-based humor funny.

☐ 53. I am often literal and do not understand social nuance.

☐ 54. I often talk to myself when I'm in a panic.

☐ 55. If I am presented with a complicated task, I need step-by-step instructions; otherwise I just can't perform the task.

☐ 56. I have trouble reading the body-language of other people, and judging intent.

Sensory

☐ 57. I have trouble when it comes to taking note of everything that is going on in my immediate environment. Normally I tend to focus on one or two things at a time.

☐ 58. My five senses are extremely sensitive.

☐ 59. If my senses are being bombarded with too much input, I will go into shutdown mode.

☐ 60. I have difficulty judging height, distance and depth.

Social/relationships

☐ 61. I often feel like I suffer from "social fatigue syndrome".

☐ 62. Socializing is harder and takes more effort for me than academic tasks that interest me.

☐ 63. I often wish there was a textbook on the various pragmatics and the unwritten rules of social interaction because it does not come naturally for me. School was lacking for me in this area.

☐ 64. I identify more with a generation other than my own (i.e. people older or younger than myself).

☐ 65. I tend to be a loner.

☐ 66. Sometimes people tell me that I am "in my own little world".

☐ 67. I am fairly immune to "peer pressure" (feeling compelled to do what others do).

☐ 68. I strongly dislike competition.

☐ 69. I love helping others.

☐ 70. I love teaching others what I know.

☐ 71. I am extremely loyal to my family.

☐ 72. Having an intimate relationship with another person is something I desire, but I would be worried about losing my autonomy, and having more unpredictability in my life as a result.

☐ 73. I usually have trouble putting a name to a face (or recognizing people).

☐ 74. To me, exchanging pleasantries with people I do not like feels "fake" and is extremely uncomfortable.

☐ 75. I can converse much more fluidly through the Internet than I can face-to-face or over the telephone.

☐ 76. I find most people bizarre and confusing.

☐ 77. I connect easier to animals than to humans.

☐ 78. People could take advantage of me because I am not assertive.

☐ 79. I often found it hard to deal with bullies because I did not have the social skills to eventually befriend them or to defend myself.

☐ 80. I tend to either really like people or hate them. With me, there is no in between.

☐ 81. People have to meet my "integrity standards" before I can decide whether I like them.

☐ 82. I dislike parties.

☐ 83. If someone is going to be my friend, they must meet my standards of honesty, integrity and authenticity.

☐ 84. I do better at individual sports than team sports.

☐ 85. Sometimes I feel my social difficulties go unrecognized because I have learned to "fake it", at least for a while.

☐ 86. Sometimes I have trouble knowing whether someone perceives me as a friend or just an acquaintance.

☐ 87. Sometimes I tend to unconsciously do things in public that are inappropriate: i.e. pick my nose, clean my ear canal, put my coat on backwards without noticing, have on inappropriate clothing attire for an occasion, etc.

☐ 88. Fashion is not exactly important to me.

☐ 89. I do not have great personal hygiene habits.

☐ 90. I always arrive on time to places.

☐ 91. I do not do well with those in authority.

Motor skills

☐ 92. I have fine motor difficulties. Using silverware, writing with a pencil, and doing things that involve use of my hands is extremely challenging for me.

☐ 93. Gross motor skills present great difficulty for me. Throwing a ball and catching it, lifting weights, throwing a shot-put, and other activities that involve larger muscle groups is extremely challenging for me.

☐ 94. I am relatively uncoordinated.

Interests

☐ 95. I have an amazing ability to stay focused on tasks or topics of interest for long periods of time.

☐ 96. I hate not being an "expert" in what I am interested in. I equate it with "social incompetence".

☐ 97. I have a collection of some kind... coin collection, music collection, baseball card collection, collect statistics on a certain subject, etc.

☐ 98. My expertise in areas of interest far outweighs my general knowledge about the world. I sometimes do not keep track of current worldly affairs because all of my time is spent learning more about my special interests.

☐ 99. I either share too much about what interests me, or I share too little.

☐ 100. I rarely read fiction books. I almost always read nonfiction or fact based books.

References

Ansbacher, H. and Ansbacher, R. (1964) *The Individual Psychology of Alfred Adler: A Systematic Presentation in Selections From His Writings.* New York, NY: Harper Collins.

Asperger, H. (1944) Autistic psychopathy in childhood. (U. Frith, trans., annot.). In U. Frith (ed.) *Autism and Asperger Syndrome.* New York, NY: Cambridge University Press. (Original work published in 1944.)

Aston, M. (2003) *Aspergers in Love: Couple Relationships and Family Affairs.* London: Jessica Kingsley Publishers.

Attwood, T. (2006) *The Complete Guide to Asperger's Syndrome.* London: Jessica Kingsley Publishers.

Baer, L. (2002) *The IMP of the Mind: Exploring the Silent Epidemic of Obsessive Bad Thoughts.* New York, NY: Penguin Books.

Baron-Cohen, S. (1997) Are children with autism superior at folk physics? *New Directions for Child Development 75,* 45–54.

Beck, A. (1985) *Anxiety Disorders and Phobias: A Cognitive Perspective.* Cambridge, MA: Basic Books.

Blitz, M., Carlson, J. and Carlson, M. (1998) Chaos theory: Self-organization and systems representation in family systems. *The Family Journal 6,* 2, 106–115.

Bourne, E. (2005) *The Anxiety and Phobia Workbook,* 4th edn. Oakland CA: New Harbinger Press.

Bradshaw, J. (1988) *Healing the Shame that Binds You.* Deerfield Beach, FL: Health Communications Inc.

Branch, R. and Wilson, R. (2006) *Cognitive Behavioral Therapy for Dummies.* New York, NY: John Wiley and Sons.

Burns, D. (1980) *Feeling Good: The New Mood Therapy.* New York, NY: William Morrow and Co.

Carley, M.J. (2008) *Asperger's from the Inside Out: A Supportive and Practical Guide for Anyone with Asperger's Syndrome.* New York City, NY: Perigee (A Division of the Penguin Group).

Carter, R. (2000) *Mapping the Mind.* Berkeley, CA: University of California Press.

Childre, D. and Martin, H. (1999) *The Heartmath Solution.* New York, NY: HarperCollins.

Chopra, D. (1987) *Creating Health.* New York, NY: Houghton Mifflin.

Cousins, N. (1979) *Anatomy of an Illness as Perceived by the Patient.* New York, NY: W.W. Norton and Company.

Cozolino, L. (2002) *The Neuroscience of Psychotherapy: Building and Rebuilding the Human Brain.* New York, NY: W.W. Norton and Company.

Csikzentmihalyi, M. (1991) *Flow: The Psychology of Optimal Experience.* New York, NY: HarperCollins.

Deford, F. (1976) *Big Bill Tilden: The Triumphs and the Tragedy.* New York, NY: Simon and Shuster.

Dubin, L. (1993) (Video) *A Lawyer Made in Heaven: The Virgil Hawkins Story.* Birmingham, MI: Weil Productions.

Dubin, N. (2007) *Asperger Syndrome and Bullying: Strategies and Solutions.* London: Jessica Kingsley Publishers.

Edinger, E. (1972) *Ego and Archetype.* Boston, MA: Shambhala Publications Inc.

Ellis, A. and Harper, R. (1961) *A Guide to Rational Living.* Englewood Cliffs, NJ: Prentice Hall.

Evans, B., Marks, D., Murray, M., Skyes, C., Willig, C. and Woodall, C. (2005) *Health Psychology: Theory, Research and Practice.* London: Sage Publications.

Evans, F. (1996) *Harry Stack Sullivan: Interpersonal Theory and Psychotherapy.* New York, NY: Routledge.

Florida, R. (2003) *The Rise of the Creative Class: And How It's Transforming Work, Leisure, Community and Everyday Life.* New York, NY: Basic Books.

Frankl, V. (1959) *Man's Search for Meaning.* Boston, MA: Beacon Books.

Gaus, V. (2007) *Cognitive Behavioral Therapy for Adult Asperger Syndrome.* New York, NY: Guilford Press.

Gerzon, R. (1997) *Finding Serenity in the Age of Anxiety.* New York, NY: Macmillan Inc.

Ghaziuddin, M. (2005) *Mental Health Aspects of Autism and Asperger Syndrome.* London: Jessica Kingsley Publishers.

Gilmartin, B.G. (1987) *Shyness and Love: Causes, Consequences and Treatment.* Lanham, MD: University Press of America.

Goleman, D. (1995) *Emotional Intelligence: Why it Can Matter More Than IQ.* New York, NY: Bantam Books.

Goleman, T.B. (2001) *Emotional Alchemy: How the Mind can Heal the Heart.* New York, NY: Three Rivers Press (A Division of Random House).

Goldstein, B. (2007) *Cognitive Psychology: Connecting Mind, Research and Everyday Experience,* 2nd edn. Florence, KY: Thomson Wadsworth.

Gregory, K., O'Neill, L. and Soderman, G. (2004) *Scaffolding Emergent Literacy: A Child-Centered Approach for Preschool Through Grade 5.* Upper Saddle River, NJ: Allyn and Bacon.

Gregson, O. and Looker, T. (1997) *Teaching Yourself Managing Stress.* London: NTC Publishing Group.

Hallowell, E. (1997) *Worry: Hope and Help for a Common Condition.* New York, NY: Random House.

Harman, W. (1998) *Global Mind Changes: The Promise of the 21st Century.* San Francisco, CA: Berrett-Koehler Publishers, Inc.

Hawkins, G. (2004) *How to Find Work That Works for People with Asperger Syndrome: The Ultimate Guide for Getting People with Asperger Syndrome Into the Workplace (and Keeping Them There)*. London: Jessica Kingsley Publishers.

Hergenhahn, B.R. (2005) *An Introduction to the History of Psychology*. Belmont, CA: Wadsworth.

Jackson, L. (2002) *Freaks, Geeks and Asperger Syndrome: A User Guide to Adolescence*. London: Jessica Kingsley Publishers.

James, J. (2007) *The Great Field: Souls at Play in a Conscious Universe*. Fulton, CA: Energy Psychology Press.

Jeffers, S. (2003) *Embracing Uncertainty: Breakthrough Methods for Achieving Peace of Mind When Facing the Unknown*. New York, NY: St. Martin's Press.

Kahn, M. (2002) *Basic Freud: Psychoanalytic Thought for the 21st Century*. New York, NY: Basic Books.

Klin, A., Sparrow, S. and Volkmar, F. (2000) *Asperger Syndrome*. New York, NY: Guilford Press.

Klosko, J., Weishaar, M. and Young, J. (2006) *Schema Therapy: A Practitioner's Guide*. New York, NY: The Guilford Press.

Knutson, J.F. and Sullivan, P.M. (2000) Maltreatment and disabilities: A population-based epidemiological study. *Child Abuse and Neglect 24*, 1257-1273.

Lawson, W. (2003) *Build Your Own Life: A Self-Help Guide for Individuals with Asperger's Syndrome*. London: Jessica Kingsley Publishers.

Lazarus, R. (1991) *Emotion and Adaptation*. Oxford, UK: Oxford University Press.

Lazarus, R. and Folkman, S. (1984) *Stress, Appraisal and Coping*. New York, NY: Springer.

Lynn, G. (2007) *The Asperger Plus Child: How to Identify and Help Children with Asperger Syndrome and Seven Common Co-Existing Conditions*. Shawnee Mission, KS: Autism-Asperger Publishing Company.

Moody, R. (1975) *Life After Life: The Investigation of a Phenomenon—Survival of Bodily Death*. New York, NY: Bantam.

O'Connor, R. (2005) *Undoing Perpetual Stress: The Missing Connection Between Depression, Anxiety and 21st Century Illness*. New York, NY: Berkley Books

Pearsall, P. (1999) *The Heart's Code: Tapping the Wisdom and Power of Heart Energy*. New York, NY: Broadway Books.

Pert, C. (1997) *Molecules of Emotions: Why you Feel the Way You Do*. New York, NY: Scribner (A division of Simon and Schuster).

Plato. (2004) *The Republic*. Indianapolis, IN: Hackett Publishing Company.

Punset, E. (2007) *The Happiness Trip: A Scientific Journey*. White River Junction, VT: Chelsea Green Publishing Company.

Reeve, J. (2004) *Understanding Motivation and Emotion*. New York, NY: John Wiley and Sons.

Robbins, T. (1997) *Unlimited Power*. New York, NY: Fireside.

Rogers, C. (1961) *On Becoming a Person: A Therapist's View of Psychotherapy*. Boston, MA: Houghton Mifflin.

Rourke, B. (1989) *Nonverbal Learning Disabilities: The Syndrome and the Model*. Upper Saddle Rv, NJ: Prentice Hall Inc.

Rufus, A. (2003) *Party of One: The Loner's Manifesto.* New York, NY: De Capo Press.

Sapolsky, R. (1994) *Why Zebras Don't Get Ulcers.* New York, NY: Henry Holt.

Schelvan, R., Smith-Myles, B. and Trautman, M. (2004) *The Hidden Curriculum: Practical Solutions for Understanding Unwritten Rules in Social Situations.* Shawnee Mission, KS: Autism-Asperger Publishing Company.

Schwartz, J. (2003) *The Mind and the Brain: Neuroplasticity and the Power of Mental Force.* New York, NY: Harper Perennial (A Division of HarperCollins).

Sheldrake, R. (1981) *A New Science of Life.* Rochester, VT: Park Street Press.

Sheldrake, R. (1995) *The Presence of the Past: The Habits of Nature.* Rochester, VT: Park Street Press.

Sherwood, K. (2002) *Chakra Therapy: For Personal Growth and Healing.* Woodbury, MN: Llewellyn Publications.

Singer, D. and Revenson, T. (1979) *A Piaget Primer: How a Child Thinks.* New York, NY: International Universities Press.

Stiles, P. (2006) *Is the American Dream Killing You: How the "Market" Rules Our Lives.* New York, NY: Collins Business (A Division of HarperCollins).

Sylvia, C. (1997) *A Change of Heart.* New York, NY: Broadway Books.

Tolle, E. (1999) *The Power of Now: A Guide to Spiritual Enlightenment.* Novato, CA: New World Library.

Tsai, L. (2001) *Taking the Mystery out of Medication in Autism and Asperger's Syndrome.* Arlington, TX: Future Horizons.

Washington, W. (1996) *The Cerebral Code: Thinking a Thought in the Mosaics of the Mind.* Cambridge, MA: MIT Press.

Westat Inc. (1993) *A Report on the Maltreatment of Children with Disabilities.* U.S. Department of Health and Human Services. Washington, D.C.

Wolfe, D. (1998) The psychological center of gravity. *American Demographics,* 20, 16–19.

Wolff, S. (1995) *Loners: The Life Path of Unusual Children.* New York, NY: Routledge.

Young, M. (1998) *Learning the Art of Helping.* Upper Saddle Rv, NJ: Prentice Hall Inc.

Zukav, G. (1989) *The Seat of the Soul.* New York, NY: Simon and Shuster.

Websites

www.therapists.psychologytoday.com

www.webmd.com/news/20000809/religious-people-live-longer-than-nonbelievers

www.wrongplanet.net/postt55551.html

Subject Index

Author Index